A powerful analysis challenging
purpose of charity boards and trust
play. Brian shows with clarity a
boards should be values-led, base
strategic in nature, a partnership of peers with executive staff
without fear of respectful conflict and always forward looking.
A book every charity trustee and CEO who wants to do the job
well should read, no matter how long they have been in the
role.

Ewan Aitken – CEO, Cyrenians

Governing with Purpose is essential reading for charity trustees
who strive to improve the effectiveness of their boards.
Brian Cavanagh presents a compelling case for governance as
leadership representing a paradigm shift in the way in which
trustees see their roles, both in terms of thinking and acting
as leaders as well as feeling empowered and confident in the
value they add to their charity. I would happily recommend
Governing with Purpose to new trustees as part of their induction
and to boards planning or undertaking board development
programmes. He argues that the false separation of policy
formulation as an executive role and strategic thinking as the
trustee role is unhelpful and should be avoided. Instead, he
suggests the richness of experience around the board table can
and should be harnessed in the co-creation of strategy and
policy. This book is both thoughtful and thought provoking.
It is well researched, helpfully referenced and most of all an
excellent read.

Gerry McLaughlin – Vice-chair, Robertson Trust

It's so refreshing to read a book on 'board governance' which
is solely focused on the charity sector, and specifically on
being an effective charity trustee. I have no doubt that Brian
Cavanagh's book will be invaluable to all current, and aspiring,
charity trustees – it follows a clear structure, taking the
reader through: first principles, key relationships, decision
making, and governing with purpose. And throughout the text
there is a refreshing focus on the importance of continuous
learning as the bedrock for what the author calls a 'purposeful
board'. Cavanagh quietly challenges the reader, in a wholly

constructive way, to think afresh about board governance and to shift the balance of activity firmly away from scrutiny towards providing strategic direction. The text also offers a wealth of invaluable practical insight, which will be of interest to all charity trustees, old and new alike. You really should read this book – my judgement is that you'll be a better trustee for having done so.

Andrew Burns – Chair, Scottish Council of
Voluntary Organisations

Governing with Purpose is an incredibly valuable resource for anyone new to the world of charity governance and an apt refresher for any existing trustee. Brian manages to convey the key principles of governance in an accessible manner which he brings to life through illustrative case studies. I was particularly heartened to see 'diversity of thought' as an essential characteristic of a good trustee as the evidence shows that such diversity supports more effective decision making. Whilst *Governing with Purpose* is aimed at charities, the principles of good governance are relevant across all sectors so it has wider applicability to boards. This is a book which I will be returning to and will be encouraging others to do the same.

Julie-Anne Jamieson – Non-executive director
and president elect, Changing the Chemistry

Governing with Purpose should be given to every person who applied for a trustee role and without doubt as part of their induction. It does exactly what is sets out to do – with a step by step approach to leading a brilliant board. The book is not only packed full of fascinating real life case studies and practical tips, it also delves into the human psychology of power dynamics and critical thinking. This book really will keep you engaged to the last page and reframes so many misconceptions about how to add value and be a great trustee. A must read for everyone considering their trustee commitments now and in the future.

Bonnie Clarke – CEO, Remarkable

GOVERNING
WITH
PURPOSE

How to lead a brilliant board
– a guide for charity trustees

BRIAN CAVANAGH

First published in Great Britain by Practical Inspiration Publishing, 2022

© Brian Cavanagh, 2022

The moral rights of the author have been asserted

ISBN   9781788603546 (print)
       9781788603560 (epub)
       9781788603553 (mobi)

Every effort has been made to trace copyright holders and to obtain their permission for the use of copyright material. The publisher apologizes for any errors or omissions and would be grateful if notified of any corrections that should be incorporated in future reprints or editions of this book.

Want to bulk-buy copies of this book for your team and colleagues? We can introduce case studies, customize the content and co-brand Governing with Purpose to suit your business's needs.

Please email info@practicalinspiration.com for more details.

Practical Inspiration
Publishing

MIX
Paper from
responsible sources
FSC   FSC® C013604
www.fsc.org

Contents

Introduction

I have wanted to write this book for a long time. Most of my working life has involved working with, or leading, boards. I am curious about what makes some boards effective and others not so. What is clear is that it is not down to alchemy, nor is it the charismatic leader so beloved of screen writers and the financial pages of newspapers.

So, who is this book for?

This book is for the approximately 1 million people in the UK who give their time to promote and develop civic society through their leadership of community and charitable organizations.[1] These organizations are the social glue that

---

[1] England and Wales: 800,000. Source: Charity Commission 2017 (https://assets.publishing.service.gov.uk/government/uploads/system/uploads/attachment_data/file/658766/20171113_Taken_on_Trust_awareness_and_effectiveness_of_charity_trustees.pdf); Scotland: 160,518. Source: OSCR 2021 (www.oscr.org.uk/media/4280/599187_scto421394204-001_oscr_sector-overview-report_final.pdf); Northern Ireland: unknown (www.charitycommissionni.org.uk). There are also more than 73,000 trustees in the Republic of Ireland

underpins the social fabric of our societies. The book is inspired by many years of mentoring and supporting boards and the CEOs who report to these boards. And it is shaped by countless conversations and questions from trustees and boards about what making a difference means – and how do you know if you are?

Attempting to recommend a book of governance to a new trustee, I was struck that whilst there is a vast library on governance and much of it good, it is mostly directed at the corporate sector. Whilst some of the themes are transferable, there is little that talks to the experiences of those responsible for the governance of charities.

This book aims to change that. It outlines what good governance and leadership should look like. Part guide, part manifesto, it is written for trustees and with trustees in mind. It recognizes the pressures and burdens of sitting on a board and being legally liable for the charity.

Therefore, the focus of the book is on governance and leadership in the charity sector. I argue in the book that leading a charity is both a privilege and a challenge. And many of the challenges faced are specific and distinctive ones that other sectors do not face.

A key part of the book will offer ways for trustees to be equipped to govern their organization effectively, bringing real added value to the organization and themselves. And for that to happen I believe how the role of board and trustees is regarded, and how they themselves see the role, requires a step change in attitudes.

This book explores what is required to liberate boards and empower them to operate as leaders: a shift towards a leadership and governance perspective, which I term as Governing with Purpose. I believe that to lead a values-based organization, your governance must be purposeful to be effective. And

---

as the end of September 2020. Source: Charities Regulator (www. charitiesregulator.ie/en/information-for-charities/who-is-a-charity-trustee) [accessed 8 April 2022].

throughout this book I want to share with you what Governing with Purpose means and how your board can undertake it.

It will look at what gets in the way of good governance and leadership between the board and the CEO. The book will highlight ways that trustees can become more fulfilled in their roles – for example, in their leadership rather than just scrutiny roles. So, the book will encourage trustees to examine best practice approaches in how to improve board participation and effectiveness.

I believe such a philosophy will help to underpin the leadership approach of those charged with leading, whether they be CEO or a trustee.

Why is it needed?

Since the financial crash of 2008, the public now have a better understanding of the role of boards and the impact of their decisions on companies, communities and citizens. Yet despite this, other than calls to 'sack the board' over some well-published scandal, what goes on in boards is still little understood and regarded by many as arcane and irrelevant.

Yet nothing can be further from the truth. The decisions of boards affect all our daily lives. So, whether a local state actor decides to relocate or close health services, a multinational to close its plant, or a charity to reduce its services due to a reduction in donations, all directly impact the social fabric of communities. All these decisions are ultimately made or sanctioned at board meetings. So how decisions are made and who makes them is of critical importance. And whilst there has been a tightening up of legislation and regulation surrounding board governance, there is still a need for greater consistency, transparency and improvement.

I know of some wonderful examples of governance and leadership by board trustees. By the same token, I have also seen poor examples. But above all, I witness trustees and boards wanting to do their best, but unsure about what that looks like, and often unclear how to measure their contribution.

Whether a board can measure the effectiveness of its contribution is of wider societal significance. The charity sector is an important aspect of UK economies. For example, in Scotland it employs over 100,000 people and generates a substantial economic footprint, estimated by the Scottish Council for Voluntary Organisations (SCVO) to be £5.8 billion.[2] Across the UK, it plays a major role in the delivery of housing, health and social care, as well as other key services. So, the effectiveness of charity governance directly impacts on the quality of life of many citizens who access services delivered by charities.

Yet the charity sector has not been immune to bad judgement and poor standards of governance and leadership. The response to scandals in the sector has been greater oversight from external regulators. Whilst this new rigorous approach to compliance is to be welcomed, there is a concern that of itself compliance is not enough to bring greater consistency to governance.

The interconnectedness between citizen donations, often tied to personal support for a charity or cause and public funding, places a higher threshold of responsibility for good governance upon the shoulders of those who lead charities. And as the sector continues to seek financial security and greater fiscal independence, there is even more reason for ensuring good governance as a strategic priority.

It is in response to increased scrutiny and greater regulatory demands that boards need to get ahead of the curve and focus on their leadership and governance role.

Re-imagining the value of trustees

I have been lucky in my life to lead many organizations and boards and have learned from others and from many

---

[2] SCVO, 'Guide to working and volunteering in the sector', 2021. Available from: https://scvo.scot/policy/guide-to-working-and-volunteering-in-the-sector [accessed 8 April 2022].

mistakes. My first adult experience in governance was shaped by decisions over whether or not to place vulnerable young people in residential care. As a lay person in a professional-led system, I saw my role to test the efficacy of the proposals and whether they were in the best interests of the young person. It was a great grounding in how the value of the lay person combined with professional/technical knowledge is a good basis for decision making.

That experience stood me in good stead. And after what seems a lifetime on committees and boards, I now spend a lot of time mentoring boards. However, being a good trustee is not just about knowing your roles and responsibilities; it is about how you carry them out. But above all knowing your own 'why'. Why this organization? And what do you believe you can bring and add value to? Yet at the same time, being a trustee on a board should be an enjoyable and rewarding experience.

I am passionate about the value that you as trustees bring to the governance of charities. Your knowledge, your expertise or lived experience, combined with the professionalism of the CEO and senior staff, provide the potential for dynamic leadership and effective governance.

It can be a demanding and time-consuming role. As in any other role, boards and trustees need support to be the best they can be. Good boards are ambitious to get better, to become more effective, and above all to enjoy the experience. For trustees to know that their commitment and contribution are making a difference and that they are an asset to their chosen charity can be a fine reward for their endeavours.

Ultimately, I would like this book to stimulate your thinking, and for you to look afresh at your own leadership as one of governance.

I hope you enjoy it.

Part 1

First principles

1 Governing with Purpose

Introduction

So, what is Governing with Purpose and what does it mean for board trustees? Before diving into the answer, let us look at a common view of what being on a board is.

With almost a million trustees governing charities across the whole of the UK, there is a sizeable audience who want to know the answer, or who already know it. It is a truism that being a trustee on a charity board should be simple. So, if boards and their trustees carry out these functions well, their charity will continue to thrive. Yet simple does not mean easy.

And if it were that simple there would be no need for the plethora of codes and legislation emanating from governments, guidance from organizations such the Institute of Directors and the National Council for Voluntary Organisations, and studies of good governance practice from academic institutions across the developed world, most notably the US. Indeed, academic studies of boards, combined with anecdotal evidence from trustees themselves, highlight that boards are often unclear about their role and how to perform good governance effectively. And, for those who do seem clear about their role, they often have too narrow a view, and one that is focused on a particular theme.

Chapter aims

The aim of this chapter is to explain what the concept of Governing with Purpose means, how it can assist you as trustees to focus on your key roles and get to know your 'why'.

The role of the board

According to Patrick Dunne, it is best described as follows:

> The purpose and role of the Board is to ensure that there is the right purpose, vision and strategy, as well as the right resources and the right governance to achieve them.[1]

This definition encapsulates what the role is; the challenge is how trustees can be effective in ensuring the functions can be carried out. In essence, the stuff of governance. So, what do these words actually mean? Dunne helpfully gives an expanded definition of what the right strategy means:

- There is a good process for formulating and adapting strategy that covers ambition and risk.
- The agreed strategy is being implemented and monitored for divergence.[2]

In terms of resources, that means that your charity has enough to deliver the agreed strategy, which usually means obvious matters such as staff, assets and purpose. In terms of governance there is a plethora of definitions on how organizations are directed and managed.

What is in a name?

There is a veritable lexicon for members of boards. The terms board directors, board trustees, board members and members

---

[1] Patrick Dunne, *Boards*, 2021, p. 2.
[2] Patrick Dunne, *Boards*, 2021, p. 7.

of the management committee are used to describe the people who govern charities. Throughout this book only the term trustees or board trustees will be used to designate those who are appointed to sit on the board.

Similarly, in relation to those employed to manage the charity, the terms used will be CEO and executive to designate senior staff who support and work under the CEO, and who may on occasions present to the board.

The board will be designated as the board or the board of governance.

Governing as a trustee

Sitting on the board of a charity and discussing the agenda in front of you, it suddenly becomes clear that you are responsible for the governance of an organization. Whether at your first meeting or your fortieth, that realization of responsibilities always hits home. You are accountable in a civic and also in a legal sense. As a trustee of a charity you have obligations under various pieces of legislation. To fulfil your role as trustee you have four key functions.

Purpose and vision and values

The purpose is the 'reason for being' of the charity. The board needs to check whether that purpose is still relevant, and test policy, development, and so on, against the yardstick of achieving the purpose. Knowing where you are going makes it easier to get there. Vision is crucial and the board needs to focus on the big picture so that the charity can make the impact that it desires. The values guide the charity. The board has a particular responsibility to uphold the values by putting them into practice.

Delegating to management

Delegating operational decisions to management allows for better operational effectiveness. The function of the board is to ensure that there are clear processes for delegation and rigorous oversight. This will be discussed further in Chapter 6.

Ensuring accountability

The core function of the board is to ensure accountability for the overall financial and operational performance of the charity. The board has a fiduciary duty to ensure that finances are used solely for what is laid down in the purpose of the charity. This is scrutinized by the board through the committee system and performance appraisal of the CEO. This will be further discussed in Chapter 8.

Key attributes of good trustees

There are seven attributes that trustees should have or aspire to having to enable them to Govern with Purpose. These will improve your board's effectiveness and through that encourage you to recognize your contribution and the value it brings.

Taking the helicopter view

The ability of trustees to see issues from different perspectives and positions from the CEO and executive brings real added value to board governance. It enables trustees to take a more strategic view and is a competence that trustees should value.

Diversity of thought

The ability to have your own thoughts and an approach to thinking through decisions is crucial to good board governance. Diversity of thought better equips trustees in dealing with matters that don't fit neatly into binary either/or approaches that can bedevil board decision making.

Debating and challenging

Trustees need to show a willingness to engage in debate and to test, assess and challenge not just the CEO and executive team, but fellow trustees. The temptation not to state your views can lead to groupthink.

Managing dilemmas

Trustees have the ability to drive the board forward yet at the same time keep it under measured control. Therefore, trustees are both responsible but detached and able to deal with the immediate and abstract.

Staying strategic

As a trustee, recognize that you have a key role in directing and guiding the strategic focus of the charity, not just critiquing or scrutinizing it.

Developing a leadership style

As a trustee your overarching responsibility is a leadership and governance one. So develop a way of leading that you are comfortable with and which plays to your strengths and interests.

Valuing the question

For trustees, realizing the value and power of the question will result in you enjoying your board experience more as you will be more effective. Well-placed questions have a variety of benefits, whether in terms of performance or improving the decision-making options. Either way, this is a critical competence that trustees should have.

Governance challenges

Many trustees, when asked what their roles and responsibilities are, would answer based on what was outlined earlier in the chapter. And this is consistently expressed as scrutiny, strategy and accountability.

In essence, the stuff of governance and its role cannot be underestimated. However, that functional approach regarding themes such as scrutiny as the 'bread and butter' has its dangers and can create tensions between trustees and the CEO/executive team in how their roles are perceived.

Much of this tension can stem from a 'clash of cultures' between the CEO and Chair/board members' responsibilities. This often manifests around the set pieces of budgets and organizational performance, where board members focus on holding the CEO to account. Whilst this is an important role, unless board members have thought about what they want to achieve beyond holding the CEO to account, it can often descend into a 'memory test' from which the CEO is likely to emerge unscathed.

The reality is that the CEO has greater knowledge of the detail and grasp of the operational performance of the organization because it is their core job to direct the organization in line with the board's wishes. Such quizzing on the detail, and a result of an overemphasis of holding the CEO to account for what has happened, means that trustees spend most of their time looking backwards, wise after the event.

It is important to avoid the impression that boards who focus on their roles and responsibilities through rigorous assessment are not diligent. Nothing could be further from the case. However, building a Governing with Purpose board is not just about honest endeavour from trustees; it is about operating in a space in which you as governors and leaders are able to be highly effective.

It is here that the division between CEO and executive team and trustees is very sharp. The executive team can point to specific targets in, for example, winning of tenders and external assessment as measures of how they are making a difference, professionally speaking. For trustees it can be more difficult. You are enablers and not actioners. One of your challenges is to be able to recognize that while the CEO and executive team can point to their successes, trustees often achieve success by proxy, which means it can be hard to measure the actual difference they make.

However, for some trustees this need to demonstrate that a difference is being made can tempt them and the board to focus on process issues such as staff complaints and other operational details to measure achievement. Whilst understandable, entering into operational matters is not the role of trustees.

It distracts from the bigger picture and limits the amount of power of the board as a governing body.

So, the effort is not in doubt, but the misapplication of energy and time on operational detail, rather than strategic direction, surrenders both power and influence. It can also promote dissatisfaction from trustees about their role, often expressed as 'I don't really know if I am making a difference'.

It is a good question and one that board trustees need to ask of themselves on a regular basis. As well as asking the question, board members need to be able to measure what making a difference means to the board, and of course to themselves. One of the challenges board members can face is providing meaning to what they do and being able to demonstrate that value in a way that they can relate to.

One of the reasons why trustees drift into process and don't concentrate on purpose is that process issues are tangible and can be measured and touched. This, combined with 'looking backwards' conducting scrutiny duties, can give a sense of relevance and meaning to their role.

Governing with Purpose

Let's now answer the question posed at the beginning of this chapter. What is Governing with Purpose?

Governing with Purpose marks a departure from the traditional board where there is a separation of powers between the CEO/ executive team and the board trustees, often expressed in terms of their scrutiny and strategy duties. Governing with Purpose goes beyond that functional role and is influenced by the typology of boards identified by Ram Charam of ceremonial/ traditional, liberated and progressive.[3]

- That governance and leadership is the primary role of the board trustees.

---

[3] Ram Charam, *Boards that Deliver*, 2005, p. xi.

- That trustees play a critical role in policy and strategy development.
- That trustees are the guardians of the purpose – the keepers of the flame of the charity.
- That trustees have a key leadership role as advocates, ambassadors and influencers.
- That boards are committed to the principle of continuous learning and development for trustees.

Now more than ever, and in light of the COVID-19 pandemic, where the resilience and capabilities of boards were stretched like never before, a new approach to governance is required. Not that the current system was unsuccessful; indeed, by and large boards handled their response to COVID-19 well.

Rather, the unpredictability of such an event shook organizations to the core. And the growing climate crisis, again with the potential for unforeseen events, heightens the need to strengthen governance systems. Dealing with the complexities of future and unpredictable external events requires boards to utilize all the skills of people sitting at the board table and in the executive team.

A Governing with Purpose board has a very effective method of policy formulation and decision making in that it encourages engagement with trustees and the CEO/executive team at the earliest opportunity to come up with better solutions. Governing with Purpose demonstrates a step change in the way that trustees become proactive in developing their leadership responsibilities.

It challenges the concept of traditional boards that the governance function often subdivided into the themes of scrutiny and strategy, which is what can be regarded as the 'bread and butter' of the trustees' role. Instead, it promotes the concept of governance as leadership and through the use of the model of generative thinking (Chait et al.),[4] it develops generative work between the trustees and the CEO/executive as a fluid unit of interplay and interconnection across the traditional binary divide or responsibilities.

---

[4] Richard P. Chait et al., *Governance as Leadership*, 2005, p. 79.

Such an approaches liberates and empowers trustees to bring their expertise and their lived experiences to become more engaged at an earlier stage on the things that count, of which ethos and purpose are essential.

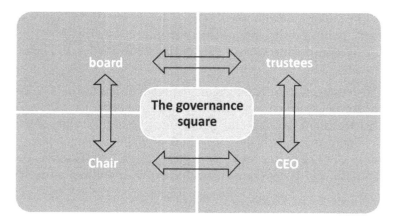

Figure 1.1: *The governance square*

The governance square graphic highlights the interconnectedness of all the key places that typifies Governing with Purpose. This brings together all the key players and demonstrates a much more effective mode of policy formulation and strategy development. The double-facing arrows highlight the processes by which respective expertise can be shared for better outcomes.

Adopting the Governing with Purpose approach

So, how can the board and trustees deal with the challenges outlined earlier and operate as a Governing with Purpose board?

As previously indicated, Governing with Purpose is about the board and trustees recognizing that their primary role is a governance and leadership one. In relation to the four functions, the area of purpose mission and values is the most important one for the board and the charity. Trustees have a distinctive role to play in ensuring that the ethos of the charity is a live and active set of values that everyone signs up to and practises.

As keepers of the flame, as a trustee you have a special responsibility to ensure that the ethos of the charity is tangible and living, and that it is expressed in the way the board and the staff act out the values. Demonstrating these values is a tangible example of a Governing with Purpose board.

At the outset, trustees need to have the personal confidence to exercise both independent thought and action. This is critical for setting the direction of the charity, a role for you as a board trustee.

Trustees need to be comfortable with debating and challenging the formulations or suggestions of executive teams. It is through this testing, assessing and questioning that the value of the lay board member is demonstrated, and the decision-making process is the better for it. Being critical, yet constructive, is a key skill, and boards need development to help them hone it.

Work needs to be put in to develop the connection between policy formulation and strategic thinking decisions, realizing that members have a role and contribution to make in both spheres. Avoid the false separation of policy formulation as an executive role and strategic thinking as the trustee role.

In the wider context, these individual development needs all bring out the importance of the board not being too uncomfortable with being both critical and constructive. It needs to work as a reflective, assessing and debating decision-making group. For that to work effectively, behaviours need to be established, agreed and understood.

Why is this important? Well, boards are often full of egos; board trustees, especially in the charity sector, are committed to the organization's purpose and have a desire to take action or make things happen. So, getting the balance right of driving forward at the same time as ensuring prudent control of the organization can be a heady mixture! Hence, an understanding of 'how' to work together and 'what' to work on is an important part of healthy board dynamics.

Yet where is the learning by the board members on how to change that dynamic? Board trustees need to move from an engineering solution, i.e. something needs to be fixed, to a horticultural solution, i.e. tending and growing – a better metaphor for Governing with Purpose, which requires relationships based on respect.

Many trustees, when asked what their roles and responsibilities are, would provide a variant based on the following. Their answer would include scrutiny, assessing risk, strategic direction, and holding the CEO to account on organizational performance. The stuff of board governance.

The need for the governance function to be effective can be evident in where board members understand their role in relation to strategy and oversight, tangible roles that are easy to understand. And when these are accompanied by large documents, they provide things that trustees can 'get their teeth into'. Yet if the challenges faced by the board are not explicitly identified, trustees can be unsure about where to start and where to look to deal with the matter.

As trustees, you need to be aware of the desires of the executive team to get you to focus on their agenda. It often attempts to get 'buy-in' on the executive agenda, leaving little space for what you would like the board to focus on. Again, this has an impact on whether trustees feel if they are making a difference. Knowing why you are there helps the board put the agenda of the executive team in context.

Knowing your 'why'

Knowing your purpose and keeping focus is critical for a Governing with Purpose board. Yet for trustees this can be difficult with many different demands placed upon them, from dealing with an emergency crisis meeting over funding to trying to grapple with board papers that don't really address the issue.

As trustees, in short, you need to know your 'why': why you joined a particular charity and what you want to achieve is crucial. This may be buttressed by a particular skill/attribute or experience you want to bring to your board role. Knowing your 'why':

- Will help you navigate the competing demands on your time and focus your energies on where you can make the most impact. The clarity of focus enables you to be effective and it is also a good role model for fellow trustees.

- Will assist you in practising the values of the charity in your behaviour towards fellow trustees and others during times of stress.
- Will prevent you from making decisions due to personal motivations rather than to help the charity to achieve its purpose.
- Will enable you to challenge the behaviour of disengaged or disconnected fellow board members.

Competing and conflicting information is coming at you all the time. Therefore it is important that you keep on track.

Keeping on track

One way to keep yourself on track is to develop your own 'manifesto'. It should highlight what you want to achieve and how to go about it. The manifesto should state how you will be behaving and how you will participate. The more explicit you are, the easier it is to help keep track of your priorities and your board goals and role. As a result, you are more likely to engage in the purpose rather the process questions. So, at the start of your board appointment or new board year, set out:

Goals	Specific examples of what you want to achieve.
Priorities	Specific areas you wish to focus on.
Interests	What things you wish to concentrate on, e.g. strategy, policy decision – financial risk.
Behaviour	How you will interact in the boardroom – and tie this to the seven attributes.
Development	What areas do you want to strengthen in terms of skillset?

Conclusion

Governing with Purpose is designed to provide trustees and boards with a new way to lead and govern, suggesting that trustees make leadership and governance their primary role. Filling that role will help trustees have a clearer sense of making a difference and a better way to measure their own satisfaction.

The chapter highlighted many of the challenges that boards and trustees face, and what is clear that the business-as-usual model is not sustainable for boards, nor is it sufficient for trustees who want their skills to be exercised to the full.

Finally, knowing your 'why' is critical to ensuring that you, as a trustee, stay on track, combining personal goals with strategic governance objectives to be the best trustee you can be.

2 What does good board governance look like?

Introduction

So, what defines a good charity board? Spoiler alert: the answer is not one that finishes meetings on time! In a response to a Royal Commission on trade union reform, Harold Wilson famously dismissed boards and committees with the line 'they take minutes and waste hours'.[1]

And whilst that dismissive tone may not accurately reflect board performance, much of the language used by commentators and sometimes by those who populate these boards is at best neutral. Less endearing pictures are also painted. Many of us are familiar with the stereotype, even if it is not our own experience.

Even the way that some trustees talk about their next board meeting with feelings extending from frustration to a heavy heart indicates that even in the best of charities, governance can be seen as tedious and tiresome. Some of that frustration can be due to unreal expectations about what a board meeting

[1] The Royal Commission on Trade Unions and Employers' Association, 1965–68. HMSO. Harold Wilson was speaking in 1969.

should be like. Certainly, the fictional representation of the board as a constant source of fireworks and intrigue is well short of the mark.

The work of governance is not one of high drama, but rather one of application and seriousness of purpose. Yet at the same time, being involved in a cause organization should be a source of joy and satisfaction, rather than a chore.

Chapter aims

This chapter will set out the foundations of what good charity governance looks like. It will highlight the key components critical to good governance and demonstrate how you as a trustee can enjoy the experience.

What is governance?

Before going on to address what good governance is, let's define what governance actually is. According to Chris Cornforth, 'Governance is the systems and processes concerned with ensuring the overall direction, effectiveness, supervision and accountability of an organisation'.[2]

He goes on to codify this as follows

- Direction – providing leadership, setting strategy and being clear about what the organization is aiming to do.
- Effectiveness – good use of financial and other resources to achieve desired outcomes.
- Supervision – establishing and overseeing controls, risk management and monitoring performance.

---

[2] Mair Rigby, 'Where does governance start and end?', 2020. Available at: https://charitygovernancecode.medium.com/where-does-governance-start-and-end-954a51090659 [accessed 8 April 2022].

Good board governance

The essence of good board governance is a convergence of two approaches. One is led by the CEO and executive team, responsible for day-to-day operations which reports to the board. The other is this executive expertise shared with the wider experience of board trustees as the basis for effective decision making. At the heart of this is the board meeting itself. It provides a forum for trustees to interrogate information, challenge the assumptions of the executive team, and balance the demands of growing with exercising prudent control of resources.

Group dynamics

So, what does good governance look like? It is dependent on three core activities that boards and trustees should focus on, namely group dynamics, substantive issues and decision-making structures. We will look at each in turn.

The first key element is group dynamics. Group dynamics play a major part in the quality of board governance. How the board interact with each other is critical to how 'good' the governance is. After all, these behaviours set the tone for how the board 'does things' and those behaviours, good and not so good, permeate the rest of the organization.

These dynamics go to the core of the governance decision-making circle. This encompasses the board, Chair and CEO. Each have a relationship with each other. And it is in this circle that all the key issues, behaviours, attitudes and roles are acted out. Therefore, when re-imagining and recasting the board as one Governing with Purpose, committed to governance as leadership, it is here that much of the work is to be done.

In creating the conditions for good governance and healthy group dynamics, let's start by acknowledging one of the issues that can get in the way: the nature of the asymmetrical engagement of different board actors. Essentially it goes like this. The CEO and executive team are engaged with the charity on a daily basis, managing and dealing with the operational functions. They have a detailed grasp of issues and are always 'on'.

By contrast, as a board your activity is more episodic, e.g. meetings on a monthly basis. You are only 'on' for those specific actions. In the case of the Chair, depending on their personal style that may include weekly contact with the CEO.

Here is a specific example. Whilst interviewing trustees as part of the research for this book, some indicated that each board meeting was like 'starting over' as there had been little engagement between meetings. For their part, some CEOs expressed frustration at waiting on the board getting 'up to speed' on issues that had been exhaustively planned by the executive team, yet often took two board meetings to resolve. It is important to recognize that an appearance of operating to different rhythms can have an impact on group dynamics and thus board relationships.

Case study

Caroline was pleased that the board had agreed to discuss her ideas on delegated decision making. She had pushed for it since becoming CEO a year ago. It was clear to her that as the charity grew, the decision making within the organization was clunky and slow. Too many decisions required her sign-off, and there were a number of decisions that required board approval for legacy reasons. She was excited at the prospect of taking the board through her proposals.

Caroline had designed a tiered decision-making system that started with all operational decisions being overseen by her. There was planned delegation to senior staff, with a financial limit and spending powers aligned to their role. Short-life working groups would replace internal committees. The opportunity to speed up decisions and free up valuable staff time was significant. So she had a spring in her step when Declan, the Chair, introduced her.

The presentation went well, but very soon the session descended into detail. Trustees wanted to discuss the levels of financial limits, and wanted to start writing revised instructions to staff. When Declan as Chair began to write up headings on the whiteboard, Caroline could feel her energy drain away. The meeting ended three hours later, with nothing agreed. She had been preparing for a week and there were rumblings from staff and trade unions stating that the current level of decision making was unsustainable and causing stress. Declan said he thought the meeting had gone well – and trustees had offered help with designing the detailed delegation information for staff. Caroline's heart sank – all the work on the presentation and none of the strategic points agreed – and wondered if she was in the right job.

The way to resolve such an issue first rests with the Chair in ensuring alignment between board business expectations in advance of any board meetings and the purpose of these meetings. But at the heart of it is trustees and the executive team recognizing and respecting their different, but mutually reinforcing, roles as key to good governance. That requires clarity on who does what, set against the purpose of the charity.

The relationship between the Chair and CEO has a significant bearing on much of what has been outlined above. How it functions is the key dynamic that drives the rest of the group. Chapter 5 looks at that relationship in more depth. Suffice it to say that it does not mean that the board cannot function if that is a poor relationship. However, it can make some of the processes more contested than if the relationship is a secure and open one.

Nor does it mean that the only relationship is the one between the Chair and the CEO. After all, the rest of the board and, to some extent, the executive team, can both affect that relationship – for example, through negative behaviours that place a strain on the Chair/CEO. And in areas of tension between the Chair and CEO, other trustees, especially office bearers such as the Vice Chair, should intervene to address the issue and manage a resolution.

The nature of the personalities on the board itself has an impact on group dynamics. Getting a balance of personalities, competencies and capabilities is not an exact science. Few Chairs are in the fortunate position to be able to select all the board at one time. And unless a board has term limits, board turnover will be reactive not planned. Thus, it is important that the Chair seeks to adopt a learning board approach to enable trustees to operate to their full potential and ensure that their skills are fully utilized. Chapter 11 will explore this in more detail.

Trustees come in all types. However, a balance of different types can aid good governance, for example:

- *The collegiate* – keen to seek consensus with an approach to open communication and information sharing.
- *The strategist* – wants to focus on the big picture and plan in three- to five-year time spans. Good at analysing plans from the executives.
- *The granularist* – ability to rigorously analyse the effectiveness of proposals and operational numbers with strong grasp of detail. Most effective in the committee rooms.
- *The risk averse* – reluctant to make decisions without extensive analysis and engagement with executive teams.
- *The maverick* – asks and challenges the assumed position. Helps others to become more curious and question more.
- *The technician* – knows more about processes than the executive team. Important in complex organizations where the executives use their operational dominance to 'bully' non-executives.
- *The cause person* – holds the moral compass of the board and reminds the membership that there is a higher purpose in which they are engaged.

Yet concentration on the types highlighted, whilst important, of itself offers no guarantee of good governance, nor the principle of governance as leadership. The key to good group dynamics is a set of attitudes and behaviours conducive to a curious, engaged and committed board. In the first instance, these behaviours need to come from the Chair mirroring them to the board and at the same time encouraging ownership by the board.

Secondly, the Chair should talk about the 'way we do things here' as well as meeting regularly with trustees and getting to know their 'why' – i.e. their motivation for being on the board, which is valuable for the Chair to learn.

Thirdly, all trustees have a 'duty of care' to the charity and should call out inappropriate behaviours that militate against the best interests of the charity. As a trustee, your role is vital in defining, maintaining and reviewing the quality of the governance of the whole organization, which includes fellow trustees.

Substantive issues

The second key element of good governance is how the board deals with substantive issues. As has already been stated, the nature of group dynamics can have a significant impact on the quality of governance. And for boards to be focusing on their primary role, i.e. governance and leadership, trustees need to focus on substantive matters.

Some of my experience in working with boards and CEOs mirrors a criticism by both trustees and CEOs, which is that boards are not devoting enough time to topics and issues that really matter. This is backed up by empirical evidence from BoardSource:

> Board meeting time is a precious and limited resource, with most boards meeting for two hours or less each time they come together… and executives currently report that 38 percent of all meeting time is spent on routine reporting. This reality may be limiting the boards' ability to fully leverage its leadership role to benefit the organization and its overall performance.[3]

There is a place for that scrutiny. But scrutiny after the fact can be a powerless place for trustees to be, and a safer space for the CEO and executive team. If not planned and thought through, it can often descend into a questioning process that

---

[3] BoardSource, *Leading with Intent: 2017 National Index of Nonprofit Board Practices*. Available at: https://leadingwithintent.org/wp-content/uploads/2017/11/LWI-2017.pdf [accessed 8 April 2022].

allows the CEO to demonstrate their unrivalled knowledge and experience of the organization. *Thus, too often discussion of important matters such as strategy, external threats, succession strategies and developing influence are squeezed in at the edges of board meetings.* And if they are discussed, often in reaction to a crisis, it can leave everyone frustrated with opportunities for trustees to contribute unfulfilled. It is this experience that creates the climate that can, if unchecked, result in disengagement, dissatisfaction and disconnection with an obvious impact on the quality of governance. Getting this balance right is explored in more detail in Chapter 8.

So, the board agenda needs to focus on strategic, significant and substantive issues that allow iterative and rolling discussion on key themes. This provides a solution to the asymmetry challenge referred to earlier.

The 12-month agenda

The 12-month agenda is a process that allows the board to focus on the big strategic prize of setting the direction of the organization. It provides a framework that shifts the emphasis of the board from backwards to forwards. This has the advantage of getting the board to concentrate on the purpose of the organization, and not just its performance.

This approach offers a way to address the frustration shared by the executive team and trustees about how the board does its business. It provides no hiding place for the collusive behaviour that can be identified in poorly performing boards, where the trustees and the management blame each other for poor governance and not dealing with the issues.

It also has the added benefit of reducing the time spent by the board on detail. Through a structure and planned agenda, it means it is less likely that the same questions on financial performance are going to be asked time and time again. This also assuages the concerns expressed by CEOs about what a board is spending its time on, as opposed to what it needs to be spending its time on.

It allows for the agenda to be forward facing and getting the board to anticipate trends that can lead to long-term improvements in performance and/or better positioning of the organization. Either way, it breaks from the corrosive memory test of the executive team that can characterize board engagement to one where the board performs governance as leadership. And it is in this space that boards need to be, and trustees will make a real difference.

For such an approach to succeed, it needs to be understood that the 12-month agenda is not a meeting agenda or a meeting schedule. It is a way of acting as a governance board through listing specific, forward-looking discussion themes that the board and CEO jointly decide must be addressed within the coming year. How and when they are discussed are to be determined by the board. What is clear is that the emphasis is on big, strategic and significant items, and therefore it requires a different way of preparing the agenda.

This can be achieved by setting out the agenda into five broad overarching categories to cover all eventualities. These would commonly encompass:

- compliance;
- operational effectiveness, including financial performance;
- strategy;
- people;
- urgent concerns.

These headings provide the framework to set aside time for bigger discussions on strategy or the external environment. The use of information ahead of board meetings, briefings by the senior manager, the construction of 'consent' agendas, or the use of delegation to committees all have the ability to free up decision-making time to enable the board to deliberate on big-ticket items or horizon scanning on the near future.

In deciding to shift to the new approach, the role of trustees in shaping it is critical to its success. There can be tension between trustees and the CEO about who 'owns' the agenda, and whose purpose it serves.

In those organizations where there is a tension and a fear of the CEO 'running' the organization to their own agenda, this is a way of returning power to the board, and in particular empowering board trustees.

For such an approach to work it requires both trust and discipline from all trustees. It also requires flexibility to react to the unexpected. This allows you as a trustee, in turn, to play a more effective role.

Decision-making structures

The third key element of good governance is a robust decision-making structure. This can help the board focus on larger and more strategic decisions. Inevitably, the growth of a charity means it is not possible, and indeed unwise, for all governance matters to be dealt with solely at the board meeting. Other vehicles such as committees or specialist groups can enable more in-depth analysis than may be appropriate at a board meeting. And it is for this reason that committees are established.

Committees

Committees are the workhorses of board governance. They have two core functions: to enable the board to explore complex matters in more detail, and to bring deliberations and recommendations to the board for approval. *To be effective, committees require a clear remit and purpose, whether as a standing committee or time limited for a specific task.* Establishing a culture of critical inquiry, alongside robust but courteous challenge, is central to effectiveness. Acquiring the skill of asking questions that interrogate the issue, not the person, and open up discussion to allow 'deep dives' into matters all are good practices for assessing risk and seeking optimal performance and policy. Above all, understanding the power of the question and learning how to use it well is an essential skill for trustees to develop.

It is through the questioning and scrutiny at the committee that trustees acquire a greater insight into how the organization really operates and performs. It provides the space for the board to hone its governance skills and is probably where most trustees feel most comfortable, focusing on tangible matters. It also allows for developing working relationships with other trustees, the CEO and the executive team.

Effective committees create the space for the board to ask '*so what does this mean for the organization?*' questions. For that to work, the full board must give space to, and trust in, the committee. The role of the board Chair is critical here, in ensuring that the committee system has the relevant expertise to engage effectively. And that full board meetings do not become a rehash of the committee discussion.

Boards often inherit committee structures from previous boards. Others may be insisted upon by regulators. However, a regular review of the committee structure is wise, not least to ensure that they are still relevant and add value to the governance process. Boards need to accept that committees are vehicles to improve the quality of governance and other than those that are statutorily required should not be set in stone. Getting the balance right between too few and too many is a key task for the board.

Too many committees can overwhelm a governance system. Servicing the insatiable demand for information and preparing reports can become an expensive and time-consuming exercise, often generating more heat than light. It also has the potential to create unnecessary tension between boards and the CEO about the value of requests for yet more information.

At the same time, for some governance issues a committee is not always suitable. The use of short-term working or mastermind groups, populated with board trustees, senior staff, and perhaps facilitated by an outside person, could be a more creative option. Operating outside the formal structure, it can offer an easier space for future focused thinking or what Matthew Syed terms 'black box thinking', crucial to repositioning and strategic thinking.[4]

---

[4] Matthew Syed, *Black Box Thinking*, 2015.

However, as in any governing system there are challenges that militate against good governance in relation to the board and trustees. So why is it, in theory and in practice, that the place in which most of the important decisions that will impact on an organization are made is regarded by actors with disdain and, on occasions, disappointment? The following sections aim to unearth the reasons why and suggest some ways in which the board meeting can be a more productive and enjoyable experience for all.

Challenges to good governance

The heart of good governance, at least for trustees, is the committee and board meetings. It is at the board meeting that trustees act in a governance and oversight way. So how these meetings work is critical. And whilst matters such as the agenda structure, room setting and even the quality of the tea and coffee available can impact on a 'good' board meeting, there are three dynamics that can have a profoundly negative effect not just on a meeting, but governance in general. These are conflict, misguided motivation and disengaged/disconnected trustees.

Conflict

What do we mean by conflict in a governance setting? Is this a synonym for disagreement or debate, or violent opposition within a group on a course of action? It can be both, so let's look at their impact on governance and in turn how boards should handle their response.

In talking with trustees, it is clear that charity boards often find dealing with conflict a greater emotional issue than other types of organizations. As cause organizations, charity boards regard themselves as bound together for 'bigger' reasons than merely delivering better shareholder value, which can be the driving factor of private corporations.

Accordingly, the forces that bind board members are values that are deep and strongly held. The downside of those strongly held values is a tendency to place a lot of store in loyalty to the mission or 'cause' and a concomitant desire to avoid conflict. This will be explored more in Chapter 7.

Suffice it to say that conflict then is seen as something to be avoided, a destructive element that distracts from the overriding purpose. It can create a toxic environment throughout the board, which becomes low on trust and high on suspicion. And on that analysis, of course boards, irrespective of how the profit is distributed, would want to avoid such a scenario.

However, I would like to suggest that there are two types of conflict, which I would term constructive and destructive conflict. Let's deal with constructive conflict first. There are times when conflict within the board about how to deal with difficult and challenging situations, and where there are no simple solutions, can be invaluable. This is where the values and dedication to the mission of the organization will result in the board members undertaking a thorough assessment of risk, testing options to destruction, and against a backdrop of the purpose and values of the organization. And through this process, it may result in the board having to review the purpose of the organization, as it may no longer be viable or sustainable.

For example, I was advising a charity that provided support to frail elderly people to live independent lives in their own homes. This included meals on wheels, social events and activities. These operated from a local neighbourhood centre and used minibuses to pick up and return elderly people to their homes.

The charity operated mainly through volunteers, with a small number of paid staff. However, costs of vehicle maintenance and replacement, running costs for the centre and a reduction in volunteers questioned the viability of the charity.

An extraordinary general meeting took place to discuss the future. There was a passionate debate ranging from fighting on and staying true to the charity, to closing. Yet throughout the debate, despite differences, all agreed that the shared priority was continuing to provide the support to elderly people in the area. As long as the presence was maintained, even if the board had no part in it, that was an agreed way forward.

Following debate, the officer bearers sought a meeting with a national charity who took over the charity on the conditions agreed at the stormy meeting. Without that passionate debate and indeed conflict over direction and alternatives, I believe it would not have been possible for the arrangement with the national charity to be secured.

Yet not all conflict goes that way. Destructive conflict in boards can come from three broad directions. Firstly, between the board and the CEO/executive team. This can surface in a variety of ways, for example the amount of information reports contain, reluctance to answer questions, or an impression that information is being withheld from the board. Whatever is the presenting issue, it can be seen as a power play, in which the board feels that the CEO has too much influence or has independent access to other influential people outside of the board, and the board want to regard the CEO as a servant of the board. The CEO, in turn, regards the board as interfering in operational detail and telling them what to do. This becomes a simmering feud that gnaws at the trust between the board and the CEO.

The second area of what I term destructive conflict is between the Chair and the CEO. Not dissimilar to the situation outlined above, the Chair is seeking to set boundaries and control the CEO to, in effect, line manage the operational performance of the CEO through a series of instructions and issue direct orders to senior management rather than going through the CEO. Again, these are power plays that either demonstrate a lack of confidence in the performance of the CEO, or a crude attempt to 'show who's boss'. This, combined with constant challenge of the CEO at board meetings, is a toxic conflict based on power.

The third key area of potential destructive conflict is within the board itself. This can manifest in different groups of board members with very definitive views on the direction of the organization, to which others disagree, often ascribing personal criticism to those who hold differing views. Let me share a specific example.

A mental health charity was exploring ways of becoming more accountable to the people who use their services, and in particular whether service users should sit on the board of the charity.

The debate brought out strong opinions ranging from questions of competence, concerns about putting burdens on vulnerable people to thoughts on how they would be appointed. All passionately held views on serious governance dilemmas. The mood changed when one trustee suggested that the majority of the board should be service users, and the remaining seats on the board should be selected via an external application process.

This brought immediate accusations from another trustee that this was a manipulation of vulnerable people as part of a wider power play to become Chair and lead the organization in a different direction. This brought a counter charge of indifference to the plight of people with mental health problems. It got very heated between the two protagonists and the Chair lost control. Because of the dominance of the two voices, no one else spoke. After a series of no confidence motions resulted in the Chair resigning, the two protagonists walked out of the meeting and did not return to the board. The matter has not been discussed again.

The conflict moved from a constructive, if challenging, debate on significant matters. However, the descent into what became a destructive conflict meant that the board was no more the wiser as to the true feelings of the rest of the board.

When uncontrolled conflict continues, it can lead to situations where alternative views are submerged, and those holding them decide to disengage from board discussion and debate. The consequence for poorer governance because of that disengagement is obvious, and there is a negative impact from uncontrolled conflict.

In trying to manage conflict, the Chair has a special responsibility in setting out a code of behaviour – 'the way we do things here' approach. In seeking to encourage different points of view in how to initiate and manage the debate/conflict, it is essential that the Chair demonstrates leadership.

And whilst it is not the sole responsibility of the Chair, all others have a responsibility too. The Chair, who facilitates the meeting, has a particular onus to ensure the debate is robust, but not personal. At the same time they should prevent the debate from becoming personal, avoiding the unintended consequence of less discussion and honest, open airing of views, or that the discussion is dominated by the few and the tone of hectoring and personalizing becomes the mode of working.

Misguided motivation

As a reader it must be odd for concern about motivation to be expressed when throughout the book there are exhortations to trustees to discover their leadership role, and inspire and encourage fellow trustees to rediscover and reignite theirs.

Let's be clear about what misguided motivation means. This is when the motivation is not driven by the wider purpose of the charity, but rather the personal motivation of the individual trustee, whether for gain, malice, ideology or 'board agendas'.

This can be a very sensitive issues for boards to identify and deal with. Indeed, it may not be apparent to all, but it has the potential to make trustees and board meetings uncomfortable experiences. As ever, this is about context and nuance. Boards, particularly cause ones, thrive with motivated trustees who bring their energy and enthusiasm to the board. This can have a galvanizing effect on the rest of the board, re-energizing and rekindling effort.

Many cause boards seek people with a lived experience of the area/sector in which they operate, as well as professional experts in the field of their work as board members. And it is tempting for those people and their knowledge to drive the board hard and cross boundaries in being seen to 'run' the organization rather than overseeing it, the latter of which is their role as a board member. This can cause tensions with those responsible for the operational management of the organization.

This passion can turn into a belief that only they know what is best for the organization because of their expertise, regularly challenging the Chair or CEO for not providing enough leadership, and not being very satisfied by the progress of the charity. And whilst charities need to be pushed to do more, if this view is not shared by the rest of the board, there is a danger that the other trustees may seek to question whether the motivation of the particular trustee is about their personal agenda, rather than that of the organization, and that every subsequent intervention is regarded as part of the campaign.

It is when the motivational drive moves from being for the organization to personal agendas that this can impact on the vision of a good board meeting.

Let me give you a specific example. James, a board trustee of a credit union, got involved in discreet lobbying for a friend, Monique, to secure a place on the board. She was appointed against the judgement of the Chair, Samantha.

At the next meeting of the credit union board, Monique suggested seeking a merger with an adjacent credit union, arguing it would strengthen the position of both and increase financial leverage. This was against the judgement of the Chair, Samantha.

It transpires that James, the sponsor of the new trustee, was a former member of staff of the credit union that had been targeted for a merger. The merger idea was being used as a way to settle scores over sick pay.

As this story highlights, the drive to get a friend on the board was purely to develop a personal agenda, at the expense of another organization, with the board trustee using their position of influence to facilitate it. A clear case of misguided motivation.

Disengaged, disconnected board trustees

It is said that engaged trustees make board and committee meetings enjoyable experiences that are easy to chair and good to participate in. Disengaged trustees bring out the reverse.

A disengaged or disconnected board can manifest itself in different ways. I remember recently observing a board meeting where it was clear that some of the board had completely disengaged from the meeting. Often the body language is a give-away. Folded arms and sullen looks directed at certain speakers within the board implies at least significant differences of opinion, or different camps within the board itself. Either way, the negative energy is both unproductive and for some an intimidating environment in which they feel uncomfortable communicating.

This can create a toxic culture in which board trustees choose to self-censor rather than face the disapproval of their peers. The development of a board within a board where members are in 'camps' is incredibly destructive and having to 'choose' sides can result in board trustees not engaging and absenting themselves from board meetings. The impact on governance is obvious. Such an environment can also be difficult for the CEO and the senior management who serve and advise the board.

Other evidence of disengagement can be inconsistent attendance at board and committee meetings, and difficulties in sustaining full attendances with board trustees choosing other priorities over those of the board. Again, this can affect the rhythm and dynamic of the board, especially if there are new members or new staff who are starting to develop relationships with the board.

Most worrying from a governance perspective is the disconnected trustee. For example, the board trustee who has clearly not read the papers and has not prepared for the meeting. My most dispiriting experience was observing the budget meeting of a large public sector organization, when one of the board trustees proceeded to open the envelope containing the papers for the meeting, pristine, unread and untouched.

Other examples are trustees looking at their phones, checking the time and whilst present not being connected and not actively participating in any meaningful sense. And although other issues can detract from a good board, it is these human dynamics that impact negatively on the board experiences of board trustees. Conversely, however, if these dynamics are adapted or changed, they go a long way to making the board meeting a rewarding and productive experience.

Tip

As Chair, meet your fellow trustees on a one-to-one basis for a coffee or lunch on a regular basis. This should not be regarded as an appraisal meeting, but a chance to check in and connect. And as Chair always ensure you pay.

Developing good governance

Managing negative dynamics

So how should a board change the human dynamics referred to above? Finding an effective way to deal with conflict is an important starting point. It needs to be recognized that the problems stem not from conflict per se, but how to deal with it, and that it is different from disagreement. Here are a few suggestions for dealing with conflict.

At the outset, even for a group of people bound to a shared mission for an organization, each will have a different approach to conflict, different communication styles and personal values. Thus, that requires recognition of how to get involvement from the whole group.

This can be achieved by focusing on the commonalities, pointing to similar views, and looking towards how the group can build on that.

When it comes to disagreement, ensure that it is expressed with sensitivity. Disagree with the idea and don't criticize the individual, separating personalities from the idea. Remember that the impact of any conflict is dependent on what it is about, how it happened and how it is managed. In the worst-case scenario, encourage the people who most oppose each other to sit together and work out a common approach. Using these approaches will allow an outlet for disagreement, but in a way that is productive and not destructive. Ultimately, if the conflict/disagreement is so intense, it may be best to postpone any decision, allow feelings to settle down and return to the matter later.

In relation to misguided motivation, this is a much more difficult area to identify and respond to. It can come down to individual perspectives, and unless it is evidenced that an individual's behaviour is clearly venal and self-seeking, where they are hoping for personal gain, the Chair should show tact and diplomacy in the first instance to ascertain the situation.

It may be nothing more than a new and energetic trustee who wants to be supportive. That can often disrupt the established order of things rather than being something more sinister, as in the example highlighted earlier in the chapter. The Chair has a key role in addressing these matters and more effectively preventing such a situation.

Good Chairs will keep in regular contact with board members outside and beyond board meetings. It is important that the Chair builds open relationships with board members, asking about their interests, how they are getting on in the board, and what support they would like.

In addition, Chairs need to understand the personal interests and passions of board members so that this energy is productively utilized on behalf of the board and that the individual trustee feels that their contribution is valued, with their skills and expertise being used to their fullest. However, dealing with misguided motivation is not just the responsibility of the Chair, but that of all trustees on the board. That means board trustees should support each other through discussing and clarifying their roles as well as reflecting on the purpose of the charity as a way of avoiding misguided motivation.

There are similarities between the way to deal with those who are disengaged and disconnected and the 'misguided'. The key is listening to their perspective about what the board meeting is like for them. The bedrock of a good board and a good boardroom is trust. And in the first instance, it is for the Chair to demonstrate trust in all the board, to take contributions in the spirit in which they are delivered and find ways in which to reconnect with members. It may be that committees, or short life working groups, may be a useful way to get re-engagement, and these options should be explored.

However, in dealing with the human dynamics that get in the way of a good board meeting, it cannot be left to the Chair to resolve or deal with these. Whilst the tone of meetings is set by the Chair, it is important that all board members share in shaping an inclusive and engaged set of behaviours around the board table. For just as it is necessary for the Chair to show trust, the board needs to have trust in board processes, trust in each other and, above all, trust in the mission/purpose of the charity itself. It is in exercising trust that the foundations are put in place for a good board meeting.

Foundations of a good board meeting

Whilst good governance is not just about the theatre of the board 'performance', the behaviours exhibited impact on the rest of board work outside the formal board and committee structures. And since much of trustee time and thinking relates to the board meeting, getting that right is important to the concept of Governing with Purpose.

So here are five key elements that provide the foundation for a good board meeting experience:

Firstly, ensure **continuity of information** between board meetings. This can avoid unnecessary and detailed questions at meetings, which is not a helpful way to ensure good and effective governance. Instead, introduce management letters/communication updates to maintain connections between and beyond board meetings.

Secondly, operate on **a policy of 'no surprises'** between trustees, the CEO and the executive team. Allow space and time before meetings for interaction between trustees and the executive team on either questions or to flag up possible contentious matters in advance of the board meeting. This provides an opportunity for resolution in advance of the meeting and, if not, recognition that it will be raised for discussion.

Thirdly, have **a structured agenda** along the lines of the 12-month programme, and weight the agenda towards the developmental and governance items at the beginning of the meeting. The use of short life groups allows for the board to test the limits of committees and their relevance. This will create a positive energy of engagement. This should be followed by operational performance and financial items. Board papers circulated well in advance of meetings allow for better preparation and a more structured and productive meeting.

Fourthly, **realize the value of the CEO and executive team**. Explore how to utilize their expertise, beyond being scrutinized and held accountable for organizational performance. Structure part of the agenda to engage them in generative thinking around strategic aims.

Fifthly, **how the meeting is chaired** will go some way towards making it a good meeting. And whilst everyone's behaviour has an impact, both positive and negative, the Chair carries a special responsibility to set a tone. This should encourage curiosity, critical but courteous challenge, and focus on the strategic implications/direction. That means welcoming divergent opposing views, and seeking all voices rather than just the usual suspects. Above all, the job of the Chair brings clarity and affirms agreed actions.

Conclusion

The choice for good governance rests solely with all those around the board table. But it requires a conscious effort by all to be committed and act on good governance. In turn, that involves recognizing and respecting the different roles and responsibilities and appreciating the variety of skillsets and interests.

It means encouraging all voices and having a decision-making structure, for example through committees, that enables these voices to be heard and uses their particular skills to get to the heart of matter, enabling better decisions to be made.

Together that can be a powerful force to practise governance as leadership, and in this arena there is plenty of space for everyone to thrive.

3 Governing cause organizations in a regulatory environment

Introduction

Imagine the scenario. You have just had confirmation of your appointment to a charity board. You are excited about the opportunity to be involved in a cause that you are passionate about and are looking forward to meeting your fellow trustees. In advance of your first meeting, there is national media coverage of a scandal surrounding a leading charity, and it doesn't make for comfortable reading. You begin to wonder what you have let yourself in for. Welcome to the world of board governance.

You may have been a volunteer for a charity and now want to become involved in a leadership role, or you are someone in middle management who wants to develop your leadership skills through seeking a charity board appointment. Perhaps you are someone with a well-established career in leadership who wants to 'give something back'. Or indeed a person with a lived experience of a condition and wants to bring that experience to a charity boardroom.

These thumbnail sketches are just some of the reasons that drive people to sit on the boards of charities. No doubt there are more examples. And despite the variation in experiences, the common denominator is a commitment to contributing.

What makes the difference between a person who supports a particular charity/cause and one who sits on the board of governance is one of responsibility and accountability. Therefore, how you deal with the difference in roles and responsibilities is crucial. And whilst commitment and passion is important, of itself it doesn't make a person fit to lead a charity. And as a trustee it also brings legal responsibilities.

Despite the line about 'scandal at a leading charity' in the first paragraph of this chapter, the good news is that scandals in the charity sector are few and far between. The bigger challenge you are more likely to face is preventing future scandals caused by inconsistencies in board governance oversights rather than wilful attempts to exploit and defraud. Realizing that your role is not just about promoting and growing the organization for a cause you care about, but also ensuring oversight over financial and organizational performance, takes you from a supporter to a governor.

Chapter aims

This chapter will reflect on what governing a values-based charity operating in a regulatory environment means for trustees and boards. It will explore the challenges boards face and outline ways in which boards can respond.

What's in a name? As already referred to in Chapter 1, there is a plethora of names ascribed to board members. However, the responsibilities that rest with the name differ little. The sector ranges from small organizations led and run by volunteers to those employing thousands and turning over millions. However, the core difference in regulatory terms is whether they are incorporated or not. This chapter will focus only on charities that are incorporated and have paid staff.

As a trustee of a charity, it is important to recognize that your powers to act are circumscribed by legislation and regulation. Unlike a private sector company, where you can do anything that is not illegal, charity governance and action is limited to what is set out in the articles of association.

So, in preparation for discussing how the regulatory environment can assist in delivering better board governance, it would be useful to recap on what the law and regulations say. Across the UK, there are two pieces of legislation that provide the legal framework for charities. These are the Charities and Trustees Investment Act 2005 (Scotland) and the Charities Act 2011 (England and Wales). These two different laws encompass powers to disqualify boards and trustees, dealing with mismanagement and other breaches of charity law. Charities' oversight of their legal and regulatory requirements is carried out by Charity Commissions for England and Wales and Northern Ireland. In Scotland, oversight is performed by the Office of the Scottish Charity Regulator (OSCR).

In relation to the Republic of Ireland, the laws are slightly different; however, the main principles are similar to those of the UK. Ireland also has a charity regulator and enacted the Charities Act 2009 to better regulate charitable organizations.[1]

So what does that mean to you as a trustee?

The guidance (see Appendix 1) states that:

> Charity Trustees are the people in overall control and management of a charity. They may be called directors, management committee members or committee members, but the law considers them to be 'charity trustees'. They are responsible for the charity's

---

[1] Charities Regulator. Available at: www.irishstatutebook.ie/eli/2009 [accessed 8 April 2022]; Charities Act 2009. Available at: www. irishstatutebook.ie/eli/2009/act/6/enacted/en/html [accessed 8 April 2022].

governance and strategy, and for making sure that the charity is administered effectively. They must account for its activities and outcomes.

It also defines what governing is about with these six themes:

- agreeing the purpose of the charity or non-profit;
- agreeing broad strategies to carry out the charity or non-profit's purpose effectively;
- accounting for the non-profit's performance, ensuring it operates within the law;
- securing the long-term direction of the charity (furthering its objects or purposes as set out in its governing document);
- ensuring that policies and activities achieve those objects;
- being accountable to those with an interest or 'stake' in the charity.

Alongside these high-level themes, the membership and infrastructure organizations that support the charity sector across the UK determine good governance as follows:

- that compliance with law and regulation is essential;
- that an organization is well run and efficient;
- that problems are identified early and dealt with appropriately;
- the preservation of the reputation and integrity of the sector;
- that charities make a difference, and the objects of the charity are advanced – more details are provided in Appendix 1.

In terms of the behaviour of individual directors, the Nolan Principles, established in 1993 although originally created for public servants, provide seven characteristics critical for the practice of good governance:[2]

Selflessness: Holders of public office should act solely in terms of the public interest.

---

[2] Committee on Standards in Public Life, 'The Seven Principles of Public Life', 1995.

Integrity: Holders of public office must avoid placing themselves under any obligation to people or organizations that might try inappropriately to influence them in their work. They should not act or take decisions to gain financial or other material benefits for themselves, their family, or their friends. They must declare and resolve any interests and relationships.

Objectivity: Holders of public office must act and take decisions impartially, fairly and on merit, using the best evidence and without discrimination or bias.

Accountability: Holders of public office are accountable to the public for their decisions and actions and must submit themselves to the scrutiny necessary to ensure this.

Openness: Holders of public office should act and take decisions in an open and transparent manner. Information should not be withheld from the public unless there are clear and lawful reasons for so doing.

Honesty: Holders of public office should be truthful.

Leadership: Holders of public office should exhibit these principles in their own behaviour. They should actively promote and robustly support the principles and be willing to challenge poor behaviour wherever it occurs.

Now for those of you who are trustees, none of the above will be new to you. The laws and the regulatory codes provide guidance on what you 'must do'. It is clear that increased regulations and the demand for continuous improvement in governance standards will become the norm in the charity sector and as a trustee you need to get used to that.

So rather than complaining of the burdens imposed on charities by regulations, boards should regard them as a spur to deliver the best standards of governance possible. Having the highest governance standards possible is a good foundation for securing the long-term future of the charity. Being bolder in using regulations as the floor on which to build, not a limiting ceiling, is one way in which your charity can thrive in a regulatory environment. There are two principles than can underpin this: values and integrity.

Values

It is here that boards and trustees have a particular leadership role to play. Often the values of a charity are assumed just to be there, and everyone understands and subscribes to them. But are they being acted upon? It is only in their application that they become real. The board need to demonstrate in their deeds and actions the values by which the charity operates. That means operating within the ethos and purpose of the charity. This includes tackling behaviours that are contrary to values, including challenging fellow trustees if their behaviours fall short. After all, values are the glue that holds the charity together, and provide a reference point when dealing with difficult situations.

Integrity

It is here that trustees can do their best work. As a board you need to ensure that there is not an impression of one set of rules for staff and the board are exempted from them. Integrity is critical to equal application of accountability for the performance of both trustees and staff.

Inevitably, there are tussles and pushback between the CEO's perspective and that of the board. And this cuts both ways. The CEO may have to remind the board that they are not acting on their values. In turn, the board need to be vigilant that the CEO and executive team is working in a way that reflects the values of the charity.

The challenges of governing in a regulatory environment

In the context of boards working in a regulatory environment, there are common dilemmas that boards face. This section highlights three of the most common.

Veering off purpose

As a trustee, veering off purpose is one of the biggest challenges you will face. It goes to the heart of the board's credibility. So, the board must ensure that all proposals and policies discussed and agreed have the overriding objective of delivering for the purpose of the charity. By the same token, actions that militate against the purpose should be rejected. However, in many instances, the purposes are sufficiently broad, which therefore requires trustees to be vigilant to the organization 'veering off purpose', often in a reaction to a crisis. Let's look at an example.

Case study

A well-respected child protection charity was in financial difficulties and the board was facing some uncomfortable decisions. The CEO, Mo, a charismatic leader to whom the board often deferred, recommended shifting the emphasis to working with vulnerable adults to take advantage of new funding packages. The board were reluctant but after being reassured that staff were capable of working with vulnerable adults saw this as an opportunity to avoid uncomfortable decisions. However, by doing so, the board veered off course from its core purpose.

Very quickly the consequences of veering off purpose became clear. Fundraising declined sharply because previous supporters were unhappy about the change in direction of the charity. Due to complaints about the quality of its core work, the charity lost some contracts. Thus, the original gain was lost and the financial deficit grew. The board became very concerned, and some trustees unsuccessfully sought the resignation of the CEO. A year later, Mo resigned. Over the next two years, a new board, with a new CEO, returned to operating according to its original purpose. Despite that, the charity never fully recovered.

Had the board been firmer in sticking to its purpose and looking for different solutions, the situation might have been different. If there are matters that threaten the existence of the charity, it may require dramatic solutions, but veering off purpose should not be your first action.

Mission creep

Another common challenge in charities is 'mission creep'. First coined about the US army in Vietnam, it describes how a time-limited provision of military specialists grew into a huge army of US troops, with war seeping out of Vietnam into two other neutral countries. So, an extreme example. Yet it demonstrates that if left unchecked, an initial action can become a defined regular activity. So boards need to be vigilant that activity is clearly tied to purpose. The following case study illustrates the point.

Case study

A charity working with people with learning disabilities wanted to develop employment opportunities. The CEO, Luke, recommended to the board that the in-house café would be a good place to offer job placements. After a great deal of discussion, the board agreed to a nine-month trial and to broaden the opportunity the café would start to serve hot food. The beginning of the project started well; feedback from those on placement was positive. The board looked on it as a job well done.

A local building site situated nearby sought access to the in-house café for the duration of their work. The CEO agreed as it would bring in extra revenue. Soon the menu was extended to meet extra demand.

However, those on job placement felt pressured as the café became very busy. They felt overwhelmed by customer demands and the expanded menu. Soon complaints began to filter through to the board. A board review highlighted that the original purpose had been lost and the café had been driven by growing revenue and customer demands. It was not a safe space in which to develop skill and employment opportunities. The board decided to end the trial and decided that the café was not a core activity.

Micro-managing

The board has an obligation to ensure a well-run and efficient organization. But that oversight responsibility does not translate into widespread interference in how the organization operates or is managed. Often termed micro-management, boards that enter this space lose any pretence at operating in a governance and leadership way. The following case gives an example of micro-management.

Case study

A drug and alcohol project was led by a founder Chair, Gerard, who was very passionate about the work. Until the charity received funding and employed staff, the Chair and volunteers ran it. As the organization grew, rather than focus on leading the board, the Chair was a constant presence in the office, checking on the CEO and often issuing instructions to staff on operational matters.

When the CEO, Gwenn, went on holiday the Chair would 'assume' the role of CEO. This resulted in confusion on priorities as often previous arrangements with the CEO were changed by the Chair. Board meetings were dominated by the Chair, focused on detail, and every small decision was discussed by the board. Eventually the CEO took a grievance against the Chair. The board were reluctant to find against the Chair because of his founder role. As a result, the CEO resigned due to the micro-management of the Chair and board.

Conflict of interest

Conflict of interest can be a real threat to the integrity of your charity, and bring distrust and questioning of motive to the heart of the board.

Case study

An older people's care association was chaired by a successful property developer. That expertise had benefitted the association through better use of its assets, as well as building a powerful network among decision makers. The association had a piece of land with planning permission for housing. The Chair, David, pressurized the board to push through the sale of this site. Not long after the sale took place, the local newspaper discovered the Chair's partner had shares in the company that bought the site.

When challenged at the board, the Chair denied a financial interest. It resulted in an investigation by the regulator, and the Chair eventually resigned. The investigation highlighted that procedures were weak. For example, there was no declaration of interest at the beginning of board meetings and because it was not a housing association, but a social care organization, the regulations were not as extensive. The investigation also noted that trustees felt intimidated by the Chair's style, making it difficult to raise challenging issues.

> **Tip**
> The practice of starting each board meeting with a declaration of interest can be an easy way of highlighting potential conflicts of interest.

In my view, the most comprehensive and best practice models are those designed by the housing regulator in Scotland used by housing associations.[3] Because housing associations spend a lot of public money locally, contracting from large building developments to small maintenance projects, are large employers of local people, and draw board members from local communities, there needs to be the highest transparency. So, to avoid any conflict of interest, a registrar for recording interests is kept. This includes immediate family, friendships as well as contractors/suppliers in their wider social circle.

This record is regularly updated and allows boards in advance to identify any potential conflict of interest, such as family and friendship ties. It provides both comfort for the board and the individual trustee.

In comparison with housing associations, the way in which declarations of conflict of interest are registered and monitored varies quite widely across the charity sector. And whilst there are registers of interests declared by all trustees, the housing association model is a commitment to good governance rather than just compliance.

---

[3] An example from a housing association website: Rosehill Housing Co-operative Limited, 'Register of Interests', 2019. Available at: www.rosehillhousing.co.uk/register-of-interests/ [accessed 8 April 2022].

Defining good behaviour

In the charity sector, there are many motivations as to why people seek to become trustees. The diverse nature of these attributes and experiences can provide the basis for a good trustee. However, a downside of that experience is when a trustee pushes their particular worldview at the expense of the collective view of the board. Board meetings then become a vehicle to pursue a private agenda.

Similarly, seeking positions on a board purely for personal self-aggrandisement is contrary to the spirit and intent of the role of trustee. The misuse of the role for private or pecuniary interests is an all-board collective responsibility, not just the Chair's. By the same token, trustees should ensure that Chairs do not set themselves above the behaviours expected of the board. Boards who are committed to operating above and beyond regulatory norms will establish a mode of working that prevents these conflicts from arising, and if they do, will have well-defined processes for resolution.

There are two other areas where boards committed to a Governing with Purpose approach should not wait for the regulators to regulate. Ensuring the preservation of the values and integrity of the charity goes to heart of what governance needs to be about. These two areas are board assessments and term limits.

Assessments will be discussed in Chapter 11. In relation to term limits, there are wide variations between individual charities, social enterprises and housing associations. Again, housing associations seem to be the most advanced in this regard, with board members serving a three-year limit and then being required to be re-elected. Term limits will be explored further in Chapter 12.

Conclusion

Boards should regard the regulatory environment as an opportunity to build quality and excellence in their charity. Regulation is thus a floor to build on to improve quality, demonstrating your board's commitment to fulfilling the charity's purpose.

In turn, as trustees, you need to understand the responsibility of leading a charity with all its legal and moral responsibilities in a regulatory environment. Thus, the purpose of your charity is as defined in the articles of association, or constitution. These are the guardrails around which you operate. These are often very wide, which give flexibility to act in response to a crisis, or indeed to take advantage of an opportunity. However, that flexibility can have a downside as the case studies on veering off purpose and mission creep highlight. Hence the need for board vigilance and clarity on objectives, whilst at the same time not succumbing to the curse of micro-management. After all, the charity trustee guidance is quite clear in its instruction that trustees govern, not manage.

However, regulatory frameworks should not be just seen as how the board operates. They are also about how you and fellow trustees behave. And as the case studies on micro-managing and conflict of interest indicate, lack of clarity around procedures does not mean that trustees cannot do the right thing or wait for new regulations to do it. As leaders and governors, you need to set standards of behaviour that are aligned with the purpose of the charity.

The housing association model has much to commend it. And whilst it has been argued by some that the terms are too short to become fully conversant with an organization, the principle of term limits is a safety valve for governance renewal, and an opportunity to renew and re-energize. The incumbency factor has its upsides: knowledge of the organization and connections with key influencers. But it also has its downsides stemming from the incumbency factor. Trustees need to be aware of the process of term limits at the beginning of their governance journey. Recognizing that you are no longer part of the future and making way for others is an essential leadership action.

Finally, boards need to expect an increased regulatory environment. Governing with Purpose boards will be ahead of that curve, seeing it as an opportunity and not an impediment.

Part 2

Key relationships

4 *Primus inter pares* – the Chair

Introduction

The Chair is the lynchpin of the board and its governance. A trustee who also leads the board *primus inter pares* (first among equals), the Chair provides the bridge between the executive team and the board; the relationship with the CEO is critical in that regard. So, it is to the Chair that you should look for leadership in terms of Governing with Purpose.

It is often said that the role of the Chair is simple: sack the CEO, hire a new CEO and chair board meetings! Yet that crude reductionism doesn't recognize the complexity and the importance of the Chair. This encompasses both an internal leadership role, i.e. leading the board and interacting with the CEO and the executive team, and an external one, i.e. ambassadorial and advocacy roles, which will be explored in Chapter 11.

Chapter aims

The aim of this chapter is to outline the different types of Chairs and identify the behaviours of a good Chair critical for Governing with Purpose.

The role of the Chair

Despite the central role of the Chair, it is surprising that much of the literature describing the role, and what passes for training of charity Chairs, focuses on the administrative nature of the role. This majors on agenda structure, ensuring conformance with standing orders; essentially someone who presides over the meeting and ensures it runs smoothly. It would be tempting to say that all the Chair needs to do is to get better in that presiding role.

And whilst not dismissing the importance of smooth-functioning meetings, it is a diminished view of the role. Nor does it guarantee better decision making. The reality is that the performance of the Chair is central to board effectiveness.

This is determined not just by 'what' the Chair does or doesn't do. The 'why' and the 'how' are just as important. Your board cannot function without a Chair, and there is no doubt that their style and approach impacts on the effectiveness and dynamics of the board. So, whether the Chair is an active and interventionist one, or a passive and reactive one, this is a choice about how they use the power of their role.

The Chair has a particular responsibility for how the board operates and behaves. They should recognize the power and influence their position has and use it wisely. However, the key to good chairing is the emphasis on personal authority, not a dependence on their positional authority. Chairs who build on their personal authority act with empathy, encourage challenge and create the space for all trustees to participate. And above all, they set the tone for how a board should function and Govern with Purpose.

What makes a good Chair?

As Chair, you have a responsibility to create the space for trustees to become part of a confident board of governance that sees the value of the executive team to the board. Regard the Chair as a conductor of the orchestra rather than lead violin!

Much of the work of a good Chair is about setting the tone. It can be tempting to lead from the front, inspiring and driving the board. The key is how you do it. Indeed, on occasions that may be what is needed. But a board that needs to be talked at, cajoled, bullied or cowed by the rhetorical eloquence of the Chair is a weak board. (Historical examples and some contemporary experiences of world leadership show the folly of following that example.)

As a Chair your role is helping the board to realize their primary role as one of governance and leadership. It is through that repositioning as identified in Chapter 1 that trustees will add value in their role as well as achieving greater satisfaction by making a difference. That requires trustees to think and act like leaders. And for that to become a reality, the Chair needs to create a board environment that is curious, creative and challenging. One in which different voices and viewpoints are actively sought out, and all voices heard. So, the dominant voice should not be that of the Chair; instead, encourage the rest of the board to find theirs. It is about bringing out the best in board, helping them to achieve their full potential. That also includes as a Chair being comfortable working with CEOs and trustees who are more experienced than you.

In getting the board to focus on the 'why' of the charity, the Chair has a key role. As the Chair you need to be 'the keeper of the flame', which means not only ensuring that the board is focused on the 'why' of the charity, i.e. its purpose, but that board behaviours are aligned with that purpose. Therefore, that the ethos of the charity is both carried out and protected.

This approach to chairing creates a dynamic in which trustees can reposition themselves in governance as leadership. This in turn improves the quality of governance, the decisions made and the relationships with the executive team. The epitome of a confident and assured board is where they understand their role and that of the executive team.

However, not all boards operate in that halcyon world and not all Chairs subscribe to or act out the philosophy critical to good governance. As a trustee you should not be grateful for the benign munificence of the Chair. It is not enough to rely on the Chair to be the sole exemplar of good behaviours. It is both unfair on the Chair and unwise of the board. The establishment of an engaged and inclusive board is owned by you as trustees. And if such an approach is not being acted upon by the Chair, or the actions don't match their intentions, as board trustees collectively you need to push back and ensure behaviours and attitudes that are conducive to full participation.

The role of the Chair has changed. In less demanding times, there were two common types. Firstly, a ceremonial one, whose main job was to ensure the agenda was completed. Real power rested with the CEO. This Chair type was non-interventionist, with a light touch and little imprint on the organization. The other was the chieftain – in charge, dominating the organization, often pursuing agendas that were more personally driven than organizationally directed. And whilst this type was less known in the charity sector, it did still exist.

The changed nature of the charity sector means the ceremonial Chair is no longer sustainable as well as undesirable. However, there are some behaviours by Chairs that are inimical to Governing with Purpose, and which certainly negatively impact on the performance and effectiveness of the board. Trustees need to be clear on their expectations of the Chair to avoid these characteristics. There are four types to avoid.

1. The micro-manager

The Chair acting as a micro-manager is a more common occurrence in a charity than you might think. It has a number of characteristics, best expressed as exercising constant oversight on everything the CEO does. This can mean interfering in matters delegated by the CEO and this boundary breaching can result in duplication of effort and confusion within the charity. It certainly causes tensions with the CEO, whose role is to manage the charity's operational activity.

The results are organizational logjam and decisions being delayed. Effective board governance ceases to exist in any meaningful sense. Such a Chair type is toxic, and the consequences are disempowerment of you and your board, as well as a strained relationship with the CEO.

2. The colluder

This Chair wants to be in charge and regards the board as an inconvenience to getting things done. Often dismissive of board trustees, this type finds common cause with CEOs who share the same view. It regards trustees asking questions as holding things back and getting in the way. Their solution is to run a 'board within a board' to concentrate power to ensure their agenda 'gets through the board'. This takes the form of pre-meetings and lots of delegated powers to the Chair, Vice Chair and CEO. Board meetings are kept short. Extensive questioning is discouraged and persistent 'offenders' are ostracized and belittled. In effect, the many board decisions become a *fait accompli*, and participation and engagement become limited.

Of these stereotypes, this is the most dangerous. It breeds cynicism about the role of the board, creates mistrust about motives and results in disengaged and disconnected trustees. Therefore, effective scrutiny over decisions disappears. For a purpose-driven/cause charity that is bad news.

3. The status seeker

This Chair craves attention and publicity. Often with previous high-level roles, personal and private agendas are the drivers of their performance. They have a habit of taking credit for the successes of the board and organization, and are reluctant to share the limelight with others. They love the status of Chair and the trappings of power. Board meetings become an exercise in self-promotion and dominance. This type of Chair has little interest in the views and opinions of the trustees. They provide little or no support to the CEO and relationships with the charity are purely transactional.

Such a type creates a culture of cynicism within the organization and has a negative impact on the morale of the board and trustees, who wonder what they are there for. The CEO and executive team resent the 'capturing' of the organization for naked self-aggrandisement. And in turn they begin to disrespect the board for not challenging such behaviour.

This is not a dominant type within the charity sector, but there are some examples. And whilst status seekers may bring benefits in their place, especially in attracting funding and influential backers, these characteristics are often at odds with the purpose and values of your charity. And it is this lack of alignment that can cause tension in the boardroom and beyond.

4. The weak Chair

The term 'weak' can have many connotations. However, in board governance terms, a Chair who is easily manipulated or pushed around can have long-term consequences for the charity itself. In specific terms, a Chair who bows down to the loudest and most insistent voices around the board table, fearful of a challenge or a row, is one to be concerned about. This can lead to board decisions that may appeal to some but have not been tested because the Chair has not sought other views, fearful of being challenged. That has the effect of annoying other trustees, who feel resentful about the latitude given to loud voices. Bad behaviour is seen to be rewarded, a very slippery slope for relationships between trustees and the Chair. And maybe it is in the best interests of the charity for them to either resign of their own volition or that a no confidence vote takes place in relation to the effectiveness of the Chair.

These stereotypes are precisely that, stereotypes. Indeed, there are further variants, and you will have experienced these traits at some times within Chairs and fellow trustees. This immediately begs the question: what is the best type of Chair for a charity?

The characteristics of a good Chair

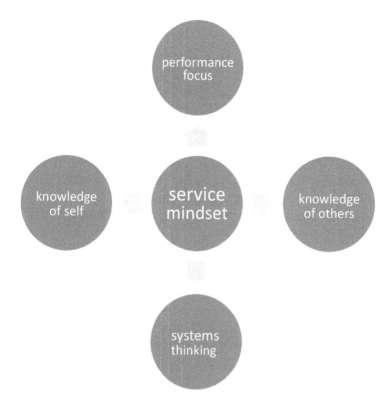

Figure 4.1: *Five characteristics of a good Chair*

Service mindset[1]

Firstly, a good Chair understands that their role is to serve the board by helping to share a good governance culture. This means creating an environment of safe but constructive challenge, encouraging diversity of thought and creating the space for all voices to be heard.

For that to happen, boards need to have a clear understanding of how they achieve their purpose or mission. It is easier to get

---

[1] Thanks to Alison Jones for providing the creative spark for these themes.

there if you know where you are going. The board Chair should have a clear vision of how the charity carries out its purpose but does not need to be a visionary leader. Rather, the role of the Chair is to inspire the board to develop its vision, as a key to Governing with Purpose.

Knowledge of self

Secondly, this Chair has strong personal authority, which stems from knowing their own strengths and weaknesses. They work on their own development and often have a mentor or coach. They recognize that they do not need to know all the answers, surrounding themselves with others who do and seeking their opinions. Working from the principle that many heads are better than one, they welcome challenge and dissent, seeing it as a virtue rather than a vice.

Knowledge of others

Thirdly, this approach to chairing extends beyond the actual board meeting. This Chair spends time with board members outside of board meetings, getting to know them, finding out their interests and how best to use their skills and capabilities for both the charity and themselves.

Systems thinking

Fourthly, the Chair forces the board to focus on the strategic direction of the charity and positioning for the future. This approach does not value the false separation of powers between CEO and board. Instead, it encourages a more generative approach to bring the skills and expertise of the board/CEO and executive team together to ensure optimal decision making.

Performance focus

Finally, the Chair is passionate about improving the performance of the board and, by extension, the performance of the charity. This type of Chair will be committed to the principle of the learning board. Eager for board performance improvement, the Chair will own the responsibility for board development and improvement. The Chair will recognize their responsibility for the board training and development programmes and understand the difference between them. This will focus on the blend of skills, competencies and knowledge critical to be effective trustees.

At the same time, a development programme is centred on individual trustees and also the whole board to create an effective working group. The commitment of the Chair to this approach and their insistence that all trustees must engage in programmes of continuous improvement brings them back to their responsibility as keepers of the flame, there to act out the values and purpose of the charity.

> **Tip**
>
> Good Chairs realize that they don't have all the answers or all the skills, yet are open to development and have their own mentor or coach to help them improve.

Conclusion

In conclusion, the Chair needs to realize they have a particular responsibility to ensure the ethos and purpose of the charity is at the centre of everything the board does. They are often seen as holders of the values of the charity. As such, the Chair needs to ensure they exhibit behaviours that are in alignment with that ethos and purpose. *Therefore, they should be seen as inspirers not enforcers.*

The Chair can have a huge impact on the way the board performs. Chairs who are comfortable in themselves will welcome challenge and differing views. That requires Chairs to be sufficiently self-aware as to how they come across and engage with the board and the CEO executive team.

How the Chair behaves can also impact on how trustees perform. Critical to this includes guiding and developing trustees to perform to the best of their capabilities, enjoy their experience and add value. This means ensuring that the Chair's key relationships with the CEO and the board are based on mutual respect and recognize respective responsibilities.

5 The CEO/Chair relationship

Introduction

In the previous chapter we established the traditional distinction between the role of the Chair to lead the board and the role of the CEO to lead the charity. The question is, whilst that division might be functionally effective, does it lead to optimal performance? The interplay between the Chair and CEO roles and the way they relate to each other is critical to the quality of governance and therefore the success of the charity.

Much emphasis is placed on this relationship and, like any other relationship, it can wax and wane but is never static. However, other than the good ones, the Chair/CEO relationship is characterized by lack of clarity on what the roles involve. More concerningly, the Chair and CEO can exhibit a series of behaviours that are unhelpful to working relationships. Here is some you might encounter.

From the Chair, behaviours such as diffidence, arrogance and micro-managing. From the CEO, typically dismissiveness, frustration and viewing the Chair as 'getting the way'. In the worst cases it can become a zero-sum game where both want to win at the expense of the other. Whilst this is not the norm, it is less unusual than you might think. And because the direct impact of this behaviour on operational performance is not immediate, it becomes tolerated, if not accepted. As a result, the charity learns to live with a dysfunctional leadership relationship.

Chapter aims

This chapter will highlight the importance of the Chair/CEO relationship, identify the pitfalls and define what a good relationship should look like.

Relationship pitfalls

There is a trend to place excessive emphasis on personal chemistry as the magic elixir that guarantees good leadership relationships. Yet contrary to many claims, liking each other is not critical, nor is being friends, though both characteristics are not unhelpful. Indeed, there are many historical examples of people who did not like each other but worked well together.

It's worth repeating that both the CEO and Chair have a leadership role. It is true that the Chair hires and fires the CEO, and in that sense is the 'boss'. But it should not translate into a situation where the Chair is constantly directing the CEO regarding operational matters. Such an attitude is guaranteed to raise tensions with the CEO and leave the Chair open to the charge of micro-managing. This view is an outmoded one and not helpful to describing the power relationship.

More challenging is when neither the CEO nor Chair are clear on their boundaries and end up 'bumping into each other' or duplicating effort on activities that fall within the responsibilities of both. This can often happen in the case of a long-established CEO/Chair working with a new CEO/Chair. It can also be an issue when an experienced CEO becomes the Chair, and still seems to think and behave like a CEO. This can be a particular challenge for the charity sector, where there is a lot of crossover between roles. That is not to say that those individuals do not perform their roles; rather, it requires a conscious awareness from both parties about what their roles are and to come to an understanding about how the boundaries are to be 'policed'.

There needs to be an acceptance that some CEOs/Chairs have no intention of getting on or working together. So before looking at the basis of a 'good' relationship, let's spend some time discussing 'bad' relationships, or where there isn't a CEO/Chair relationship. To some extent a bad relationship can be repaired; what is more of a danger to the governance and leadership of a charity is where there is no relationship to speak of. Here are two examples to look out for, which reflect different situations in the CEO/Chair relationships.

Case study 1: Dominant

Patrick was a new Chair appointed to a charity with an experienced CEO called Francesca. At their first meeting he explained his leadership style – light touch – saying that he would defer to the CEO on all operational and financial matters and would focus on chairing board meetings and stakeholder engagement. This pleased Francesca as the previous Chair tried to micro-manage her. With the Chair not being around much it enabled Francesca to focus on her role. Yet soon planned meetings were cancelled at short notice and there was little contact between meetings.

Francesca's performance review was constantly rescheduled, and when a close relative died and she had to take time off, there was no acknowledgement from Patrick. It soon became clear to Francesca that Patrick had little interest in developing a working relationship. Matters came to a head when board trustees complained about late reports, feeling that the CEO didn't respect them. Patrick supported the complaints and blamed Francesca for the problem. In response, Francesca highlighted the cancelled meeting and the lack of engagement. Yet the board backed the Chair. Soon after this, Francesca decided to move on.

Case study 2: Disengaged

From the very start, Bashir saw himself as a reluctant Chair. He knew nothing about housing, but as a local businessman was impressed by the CEO, Janice, and wanted to give back something to the local community. The rest of the board were in awe of Janice and her track record. The board struggled to understand some key issues and relied on the CEO to make the main decisions without much discussion.

Bashir seemed happy with that as it enabled developments to go ahead quickly, and Janice was delighted with no interference. However, the external regulator challenged a new development proposal that exceeded the powers of the board. The proposal was halted and a review took place, in which board members and the Chair were asked about how the proposal was signed off by the board. It was indicated that little discussion had taken place and discretion was given to the CEO. The board admitted they had little experience and decided to leave it in the hands of the CEO, whom they regarded as the expert, and the Chair was happy with that.

As a result of the review Bashir was asked to resign for failing to oversee the CEO. A new board was sought and an interim manager was sent in to manage the association. Janice was made redundant. The moral of the story is that although the personal relationship was good, there was no oversight of the actions and management of the CEO.

In both of the case studies, one of the parties certainly had a good relationship, not just at the expense of the other, but at the expense of the rest of the organization. Whilst each of the situations are different, there is a common thread. Yet at best these were transactional relationships, based on the misuse of a balance of power and at the same time a lack of any engagement with the other party.

So before outlining what a good relationship looks like, let's explore what lies at the core of this relationship. What is not in doubt, whether one party likes it or not, is that this is a relationship. So, whether this a passive and minimalist relationship or an active and engaged one, once both the CEO and Chair recognize that their ability to achieve what they want to in their roles (whatever that might be) can be circumscribed by the actions or non-actions of the other party, this provides for the basis on which the relationship should operate.

From that understanding of 'shared power' it follows that both roles have a shared external audience of funders, regulators and beneficiaries of the work of the charity, and different internal audiences, such as trustees and staff. These respective audiences seek to be heard by their principals, namely the CEO and Chair, which might result in competing and conflicting expectations. In this instance, these are about how the Chair and CEO respond to any challenge to conflicting loyalties and agendas. *The trick is finding the shared themes that sit above sectional interests. The most obvious is the purpose of the charity, which should be a powerful binding agent for the two principals, i.e. CEO and Chair.*

How the principals deal with disagreement goes to the heart of how the relationship should be conducted. If both the CEO and Chair have a measure of self-awareness and personal confidence, as well as trust in each other, it means that any disagreements will be seen in the context of not agreeing, rather than as a proxy for something else. It needs to be recognized that disagreement is perfectly acceptable and is a critical element of good governance. That means the Chair and the CEO can focus on the merits of an issue, respond accordingly and have a process as to how they deal with any fallout. Again, this not asking either of the parties to submit to the will of another, but rather to have an understanding on how to deal with unresolvable matters.

In the final analysis, this relationship comes down to trust and mutual respect. It is tempting to use each other as a 'scapegoat' to blame for shortcomings; here are two examples that illustrate the point.

1   *A CEO blames the Chair because the board did not back a request for additional staff, when it may be the case was poorly argued by the CEO and failed to convince the board.*
2   *Or a Chair blames the CEO for a high level of staff turnover but the board is reluctant to approve a new salary structure.*

Both these examples should be seen as strategic leadership failures of both the Chair and CEO, in an area where they have shared responsibility. The absence of a clear awareness of the interconnectedness of the issue has, in these instances, prevented the development of a workforce capacity and retention strategy. Yet seen through a different lens, these examples can offer a better understanding of how the roles crosscut, together with empathy for the challenges each other faces.

So, both principals need to look and act like leaders. This means putting aside petty annoyances and modelling to the board and the staff in the charity what good leadership looks like. By the same token you as a trustee should insist on such behaviours.

Definition of a good relationship

So, what does a good relationship look like? There are four key attributes that are central to a good relationship:

- trust;
- mutual respect;
- ability to manage disagreements;
- good listening.

These attributes are elemental to any relationship but are especially relevant to the demands placed on leading a charity. It is important that they mirror the ethos and purpose of the charity. And because it is rare that the Chair and the CEO are appointed at the same time, one of the roles needs to deal with the incumbency factor. All the more reason to have these four attributes on which the CEO and Chair can develop their relationship.

A willingness to recast and remake the relationship to suit the current Chair and CEO as opposed to unconsciously maintaining the approach of previous postholders is a good start. As has already been demonstrated, quite different personalities can work well together. And whilst relationships need to adapt and change in response to different behaviours, the following four key principles provide the basis of a good relationship.

Understanding of roles

At the outset, both princip[le]
each other's roles and r[e]
agreement on 'how to do th[.]
how to deal with differences
agreement of 'who does what'.

Cardinal rules

What helps to cement such unde[.]
rules, the first of which is no micro[.]   [...]air
and no micro-governing from the C[.]   [...] difficult
conversation if there has not been   [...] on this before.
However, it is important that both postnolders recognize their
respective 'must-do' roles and avoid entering each other's areas.
Not only is it usually unproductive, sometimes duplicating
effort, but it raises unnecessary antagonisms and accusations
of 'land grabs' over roles.

The main must-do roles of both the Chair and the CEO are
outlined in Table 5.1. The second cardinal rule is that both
parties must stick to their must-do roles. The two cardinal rules
allow for the development of a good working relationship in
dealing with the areas where there are shared responsibilities.

CHAIR	CEO
Governance	**Management**
Determine purpose.	Commit to the mission.
Select and evaluate the CEO.	Lead the staff and manage the organization.
Ensure effective planning.	
Monitor programmes and services. Ensure adequate financial resources and oversight.	Follow the highest ethical standards.
	Accountable for the quality and effectiveness of programmes.
Ensure legal and ethical integrity.	Engage the board in planning and lead implementation.
Enhance public standing.	Build external relationships. Support the board.

Staff development
Initiation.
Development.
Sustainability.

Boardroom	Workplace
To focus on the mission/purpose. Establish highly functioning board directed at outcomes.	Focus on tasks that support staff to focus on quality service outcomes.

Shared tasks and responsibilities
Succession planning.
Development.
Fiduciary duty.
Communication with stakeholders.

Table 5.1: Roles and responsibilities

Managing the boundaries

How the Chair and CEO deal with shared matters and respecting role boundaries is important. Disagreements should not be hidden from the rest of the board but should be dealt with in a way that does impact on the rest of the board and each other. The best place to start from is a 'policy of no surprises'.

This approach is often best served by regular meetings on a one-to-one basis between both parties. These one-to-one meetings have a number of purposes:

- provide a structured basis on which to discuss board business and strategize;
- are a safe place to explore knotty issues and areas of disagreement;
- enable assessment of the CEO's performance.

Understanding of roles

At the outset, both principals need to accept and understand each other's roles and responsibilities. This requires an agreement on 'how to do things here'. This can stretch from how to deal with differences to, in some examples, a written agreement of 'who does what'.

Cardinal rules

What helps to cement such understanding are two cardinal rules, the first of which is no micro-managing from the Chair and no micro-governing from the CEO. It may be a difficult conversation if there has not been clarity on this before. However, it is important that both postholders recognize their respective 'must-do' roles and avoid entering each other's areas. Not only is it usually unproductive, sometimes duplicating effort, but it raises unnecessary antagonisms and accusations of 'land grabs' over roles.

The main must-do roles of both the Chair and the CEO are outlined in Table 5.1. The second cardinal rule is that both parties must stick to their must-do roles. The two cardinal rules allow for the development of a good working relationship in dealing with the areas where there are shared responsibilities.

CHAIR	CEO
Governance	**Management**
Determine purpose.	Commit to the mission.
Select and evaluate the CEO.	Lead the staff and manage the organization.
Ensure effective planning.	
Monitor programmes and services. Ensure adequate financial resources and oversight.	Follow the highest ethical standards.
	Accountable for the quality and effectiveness of programmes.
Ensure legal and ethical integrity.	Engage the board in planning and lead implementation.
Enhance public standing.	Build external relationships. Support the board.

Board development	Staff development
Initiation.	Initiation.
Development.	Development.
Sustainability.	Sustainability.
Boardroom	**Workplace**
To focus on the mission/ purpose.	Focus on tasks that support staff to focus on quality service outcomes.
Establish highly functioning board directed at outcomes.	
Shared tasks and responsibilities	
Succession planning.	
Development.	
Fiduciary duty.	
Communication with stakeholders.	

Table 5.1: Roles and responsibilities

Managing the boundaries

How the Chair and CEO deal with shared matters and respecting role boundaries is important. Disagreements should not be hidden from the rest of the board but should be dealt with in a way that does impact on the rest of the board and each other. The best place to start from is a 'policy of no surprises'.

This approach is often best served by regular meetings on a one-to-one basis between both parties. These one-to-one meetings have a number of purposes:

- provide a structured basis on which to discuss board business and strategize;
- are a safe place to explore knotty issues and areas of disagreement;
- enable assessment of the CEO's performance.

Such discussions held outside the formal structured board/ committee meetings are a terrific way to get to know one another and test ideas out before they become formal matters. It is through mutual trust and respect that tactical decisions are made in the best interests of the charity, rather than being a power grab or a usurping of anyone's role.

Consistent communication

Communication is the key to a good working relationship and covers three broad areas: the Chair/CEO relationship, the CEO/ Chair board dynamic and the CEO/Chair leadership dynamic. Turning firstly to the Chair/CEO relationship, this will mean on occasion the CEO having to tell the Chair some uncomfortable truths or unpalatable facts resulting from a questionable board decision. The ability to hear these observations in the spirit in which they were intended is a measure of the relationship. Nowhere is this more important than the way in which the Chair conducts the performance appraisal of the CEO and offers feedback and guidance on their leadership style in the widest sense. This may include advice that it is time for the CEO to move on.

The CEO is often the 'face' of the charity with regard to funders and other stakeholders. If the Chair wishes to play a more visible role, it is important that this is discussed and an agreement reached about how that will be managed.

Secondly, the CEO/Chair board dynamic. Regular contact and opportunity to 'talk things out' will determine how the two principals conduct themselves at the board meeting. The rest of the board will look to the Chair, and to some extent the CEO, to set the tone for the meeting and expected behaviours. And whilst the Chair leads the board, it is important the CEO is listened to with respect. The challenge and questions by trustees can be robust, but courteous. And if the atmosphere is getting charged, it is important that the Chair ensures everyone focuses on the issue and not on the person. A good relationship means the CEO is not uncritically defended by the Chair, nor is the CEO cut adrift by a Chair who is eager to appease restless board directors.

In turn, the Chair needs to create an environment where the CEO can tell the board some difficult things about the board or the charity without being blamed for bringing up difficult issues. If the board is holding the CEO to account for both their individual and organizational performance, in the first instance the Chair should not rush to judgement. Nor should the Chair automatically align themselves with the rest of the board. Instead, air the matter further, investigate further, before deciding on what action is required, if any. A good relationship does not mean that the Chair and the CEO always back each other. It is about getting the balance right and acting in a proportionate way.

Finally, the CEO/Chair leadership dynamic. A good relationship recognizes that each principal must support and connect with the board and staff. They understand that there may be a fraught connection between individuals from time to time, which can have an impact on their relationship. However, if they can work on the basis that everything is on the table, and once discussed is left in the room after the conversation, a good relationship is being established. And that works best when both principals ignore their titles and work out how together they can use their skills, expertise and capabilities to further the purpose of the organization.

Conclusion

It is difficult to overstate how important the quality of the CEO/ Chair relationship is to the overall performance of a charity. It is not that a charity cannot fulfil its obligations; many do, despite a poor relationship between the Chair and the CEO. But that poor relationship limits the potential of the charity and, left unchecked, can create a toxic culture across the board and the development of power blocs aligned to the Chair and CEO. All that misdirected energy is not available to strengthen the organization. It also makes for a limited experience for you as a trustee.

Although the quality of the relationship sits with the two principals, the board and the executive team also have a role in stating what type of relationship they want from the principals and in tackling inappropriate behaviours. If these inappropriate behaviours are occurring, it should not just be up to the two principals to decide to act or not. From a corporate governance perspective, the board, both collectively and individually, should challenge these behaviours and seek changes in them for the good of the charity.

If there is no change in behaviours the board should, at a first stroke, remove the Chair and place the Vice Chair in an interim role. This then allows for discussion with the CEO on recalibrating the relationship or seeking a new CEO.

Part 3

Getting the balance right

6 Effective decision making

Introduction

Sitting on the board of a favoured charity or cause and making decisions that strengthen its ability to achieve its purpose is probably the clearest image of what being on a board looks like. This is a powerful image that attracts new board members to their favourite causes.

So as decision making is seen as what a board does, some analysts over-dwell on the optimal size of boards and committees for decision making. However, there are more reliable indicators of effectiveness – when it comes to Governing with Purpose, the way and the how are much more reliable indicators of effectiveness.

Chapter aims

This chapter will highlight the challenges faced by boards in the decision-making process. It will use case studies to outline the key components and techniques of effective decision making and the benefits of delegation. It will also identify the key role of trustees in Governing with Purpose.

Definition

Let us start with a definition of what decision making provided by the University of Massachusetts:

> Decision making is the process of making choices by identifying a decision, gathering information, and assessing alternative resolutions. Using a step-by-step decision-making process can help you make more deliberate, thoughtful decisions by organizing relevant information and defining alternatives.[1]

It looks so straightforward, but the reality is not always like this. Ensuring that your board can carry out decision making as defined above requires an acceptance of the inherent tension between the responsibility of the board to oversee and guide the direction of the charity, and trust in the staff to implement processes and procedures that allow consistent operational performance.

Once an organization has staff, it requires structure, processes and procedures to take actions. *It is not desirable to have every decision made by a board, nor should a board expect to make every decision.* A system of delegated decision making allows for operational functioning and effectiveness. How boards make and take decisions, and on what, will be explored throughout this chapter. This is best set out in three broad themes: Strategic, Tactical and Operational. Let's look at each of them in turn.

Strategic

Strategic is probably the easiest to define. These are decisions that have an impact on the purpose of the charity and its ability to fulfil them. And in this regard, it is vital for Governing with Purpose that the board is fully involved and engaged in the

---

[1] Board of Trustees of the University of Massachusetts, 'Decision-making process', 2022. Available at: www.umassd.edu/fycm/decision-making/process/ [accessed 8 April 2022].

process. The extent of their involvement may vary from board to board, as indeed do the processes in which they are involved.

These could include significant investment/funding decisions, mergers/partnerships and change of strategic direction. Key personnel issues such as hiring/firing the CEO and staff renumeration would also be good examples. Essentially, they are the decisions that impact on the charity's ability to function effectively and secure long-term sustainability.

For a board to be Governing with Purpose, and trustees to be at their most effective in decision making, as a rule, operational decision making should be made by the CEO or head of service. However, this can be dependent on the size of a charity. For example, in a very small charity with one staff member, a decision to increase the staff team by one would be seen as a strategic decision and made by the board. In contrast, a charity with 100 staff is unlikely to have any board involvement.

Tactical

As has already been indicated, the board should remain focused on those matters of strategic direction, explicitly linked to the purpose of the organization. The best way to separate the deciding from the doing is through a clear plan of delegated authority to staff. At a tactical level, however, there may be times when the board may want to take the decision. One of the key areas is recruitment. And whilst the board will appoint the CEO/Director, it may wish to be involved in the appointment of other senior posts that are of strategic importance.

Operational

At an operational level, implementing the strategic directions of the board is carried out by staff. The CEO is accountable to the board for their actions. The job of the board through holding the CEO to account tests the effectiveness of those actions. There is a wide range of arrangements reflecting the organizational and operational culture of each charity. For example, within the housing association movement, especially in Scotland, there are prescribed procedures to define what are delegated powers and those that are reserved for the board only. These are more likely to result in the board focusing on strategic leadership and governance.

So even in charity with a delegated decision-making protocol that defines 'strategic', what does that really mean? And whilst such a protocol could cover areas where trustees have clear control over decision making, there are always board-worthy matters arising that require an immediate response. In these cases, choices must be made over what (and what not) to submit for board consideration. Usually, the CEO makes that judgement. This is based on a set of informal norms that have evolved over time and reflect the charity's culture.

However, informal norms can still be loosely defined. The board needs to be clear on what it regards as strategic and to give the CEO and, by extension, the executive team, clarity. It is essential that trustees push back against any perceived view that the CEO and other senior staff are running the board. And by the same token, clarifying board desires and intentions around strategy creates the space in which staff can get on with operational management. Staff are then clear about what delegated authority they have.

Information flows

As Richard Hardin and Judith Roland put it, 'information needs to right in in terms of volume, structure and its focus on critical issues'.[2] Sounds clear, but in the experience of many boards, it is not easy. In the more traditional boards, dominated by an all-powerful CEO, boards can often accept the information given, leading to the decision preferred by the CEO. That 'in charge but not being in charge' role is the

---

[2] Richard Hardin and Judith A. Roland, 'Board work processes' in David A. Nadler et al. (eds), Building Better Boards, 2006, p. 89.

antithesis of a Governing with Purpose board and disempowers board members.

The simple action of providing information offers an insight into how a board functions, and the dynamic between the board and the CEO. Whether the board is a 'traditional' or a generative one, the questions remain the same. *What do boards want the information for, what type of information and how should it be presented?* On boards, trustees can have different views on what information is desirable; some want more, some want less.

We all know that having lots of information doesn't necessarily help with decision making. The way information is used in an organization can give you an insight into how the organization communicates and how its relationships work. After all, information is a source of power and how it is imparted is a demonstration of power plays.

Let me give you a couple of scenarios.

Scenario 1

A small drugs charity had its funding cut by £40,000 – 10% of its budget. The CEO provided a report and urged the board to make a speedy decision. It had three scenarios:

1   Make three members of staff redundant.
2   Shorten the hours of operating.
3   Ask all staff to take a pay cut.

Yet in this instance, the board did not start with the fundamental question, *can the charity still function with this cut?* Instead, the board complained about not knowing the extent of the problem (it was in the minutes of a previous meeting) and asked for more options. All of the options were rejected and a further report was requested. However, revised options were unpalatable. Six months later, the board made redundancies.

Scenario 2

The CEO of a community housing association presented a long-term housing development plan, which included a complete briefing, PowerPoint, maps and brochure on housing styles.

Rather than the board deciding on the plan, the meeting descended into the detail of house design and objections to specific sites. The meeting delayed approving the plan because the board needed more time due to information overload.

Learning

Whilst each of the scenarios is different, the net effect is corrosive to board dynamics. If the board is saddled with an overload of reports, it loses focus on the important issues. If trustees lack enough detail to formulate questions, the dialogue is limited and superficial. If ad hoc demands for information at short notice become the dominating factor, valuable management time is wasted on compiling information. Either way, the boards were using the excuse of lack of information to avoid difficult decisions.

So, boards cannot function effectively without quality information, but it needs to be disseminated in a way that aids effective decision making. Information builds trust. To build trust between the CEO and the board, information exchanges need to be open and transparent. In turn, board trustees need to be clear about what information they want and for which purpose. It is that trust that builds the basis for a good board. So, let us look at what a good information process for a board should encompass.

Culture of trust

A culture of trust is imperative in any information exchange; for example, with a committee system operating with a board, not all trustees will receive information at the same time. Trust is essential to ensure that no one feels left out. Similarly, consistent demands for more information as a mask for delaying a difficult decision speaks more of mistrust rather than Governing with Purpose.

Informal conversations

Informal conversations are often a good way to exchange information and ideas, including problem solving. CEOs often value the expertise of individual trustees, and informal contact can help trustees and the CEO/executive to get to know one another.

Information flow

Information needs to be seen not as something that is turned on and off, but a continuous flow. This is crucial for board committees, who have two key roles: to highlight completed matters (the scrutiny role) and to report to the full board with recommendations (the strategy role). So a key task is managing the flow of information to ensure delegated decision making works.

Board briefings

Board briefings are a useful tool to draw attention to high-level themes. They allow trustees to get up to date on relevant trends between meetings, enabling more effective use of time at board meetings.

Task groups

The use of task groups populated by trustees and senior staff can be an invaluable tool to assess quality and performance matters. This may require a different approach to information gathering and sharing to make the best use of the group.

Dashboard

The growth in dashboard models helps boards and trustees to access 'at a glance' key strategic metrics. This means that trustees have real-time awareness of trends and performance, resulting in more time spent on decision making and less on information seeking.

Obstacles to effective decision making

Even when a board has the right information at the right time, it is all too easy for decision making to be sabotaged by poor process. The main culprits are:

- failure to recognize variation in significance;
- rushing to consensus;
- the loudest voice syndrome.

Let's look at each of these in turn.

Failure to recognize variation in significance

Simply put, not all decisions your board makes are of the same significance. For example, approving board minutes is quite a different order to dismissing a CEO or changing the purpose of the charity.

As boards have developed protocols on delegation to avoid becoming embroiled in operational matters, surely they should have some protocols or arrangements to deal with the variation in the gravity of decisions. However, many seem stuck in the default position of a one-size-fits-all response to decision making. This does have the potential to limit the flexibility of response.

Rushing to consensus

Boards like to seek consensus on decision making. It can be a way of affirming their commitment to a shared cause or purpose. But that shared commitment can often turn into pressure to avoid disagreement.

This desire to discourage 'divisive' voting on matters and a resultant rush towards consensus often militates against deep discussion and scrutiny. And even in boards where voting against decisions is rare, there are examples where the Chair will state, 'the majority has spoken, let's make it unanimous'.

The implicit assumption is that unanimity is a desirable goal, which is a significant obstacle to effective decision making. It creates an environment, however unwittingly, that implies firm questioning and a reluctance to go with the majority is acting against the best interest of the charity. Such an impulse is inimical to effective decision making. It misplaces the desire to protect the charity with the duty to challenge and question.

The loudest voice syndrome

This can be a challenging obstacle. A specific example would be an inconclusive discussion with no clear course of action and trustees undecided on what options to take. Then an experienced and highly regarded trustee shares his view on the course of action required. This opinion drowns out all others and the board agree to the action suggested.

At one level this can be a decisive and welcome break of the impasse. However, because there was no further discussion after the trustee spoke, there is no real way to measure whether this was the best decision or a decision not to question an experienced trustee. In this case, the ability to sway the undecided may be a mark of practical skills but it should not be confused with effective decision making.

The mandate of the vote

It may seem strange to highlight voting as an obstacle to decision making. So, let's explore this further. Tied to the earlier point on the variation of significance, the overdependence on a binary process does not of itself guarantee an effective decision, just that a decision will be made.

After all, it can be difficult to discern what real support there is for a decision. It may be that trustees are fearful of being seen to oppose, or there are less high-minded reasons to give their support – for example, settling scores with others, and yes, such behaviour does exist in charity boardrooms. So, Chairs and CEOs should be careful not to misinterpret majority votes in favour as always signifying a ringing endorsement.

All these obstacles in their own way limit the effectiveness of decision making. They can result in 'buyer's remorse' with the temptation to unpick or review a decision if trustees feel they have been talked into or rushed into a decision.

The consequence of such an approve, recant and resile approach is the epitome of dysfunctional governance, and confused, frustrated trustees and boards.

How to make effective decisions

I have already indicated that charities need a range of tools and techniques to aid effective decision making. Governing with Purpose boards avoid binary decisions as their only decision-making process. Instead, they have a range of tools to assist in making optimal and stickable decisions. Some specific examples of tools will be outlined in the following section.

In the meantime, let's explore how trustees should engage and the extent to which they should be involved in strategic decision making.

Working with boards for many years, I am still struck by trustees, especially on 'traditional' boards, who seem to have little ownership over certain decisions. In these cases, there is a palpable sense of frustration at being kept at arm's length by the CEO, yet, at the same time, expected to be accountable for the decision when it goes wrong.

The traditional approach involves a report with recommendations drafted by the CEO and submitted to the board for approval/rejection. The board arrives at the process late with all the options usually determined before the board meeting. The board then decides their course of action, their involvement coming at the end of the process. Whilst there is nothing wrong with this approach, it does limit the involvement of trustees and access of high expertise earlier in the process. Earlier involvement might bring different perspectives and better outcomes.

Another approach is that of complete detachment from the process, with the board only wanting to decide what is in front of them – indicating that all the rest is the responsibility of the CEO and the executive team. Both of these views are a recipe for disaster, and if not, a disaster certainly for suboptimal decisions. Figure 6.1 outlines how this vicious circle works.

Figure 6.1: Vicious circle

In this example, the late introduction of the board into the process is reliant on their agreement as to the service problem. If that has not been secured this is likely to result in a vicious cycle, where either recommendations are rejected or demands for more information are made before taking a decision. It can be an ineffective and time-consuming way to make decisions.

This approach can also begin to test the bonds of trust between the CEO/executive team and board trustees, and disagreements over the core problem can lead to accusations of the board being 'bounced' into the CEO/executive team agenda.

As a first step, the board and individual trustees need to be clear about where they engage in the decision-making cycle.

Figure 6.2 Virtuous cycle

In contrast to the above, the virtuous cycle creates a much better environment for decision making. On this occasion, board trustees are involved at the beginning of the process, agreeing on what the strategic issues are.

This makes it easier for the remaining part of the decision-making cycle to focus on defining options, scoring them, consulting and then bringing ranked options for deliberation at the board meeting; this enables a more productive approach. It is likely to lead to a better decision as all options have been explored early in the process.

With trustees being engaged early in the process, there is a shared agenda between the CEO and board on what the issues are. Seeking stakeholder views of decision options gets 'buy-in' and strengthens trust in the process, as well as between the CEO and the board. And in the business of decision making, trust goes a long way. As Stephen Covey puts it, 'I submit that whilst high trust won't necessarily rescue a poor strategy, low trust will almost derail a good one'.[3]

Figures 6.1 and 6.2 highlight that there are clear lessons to be learned. The first example does limit the involvement of board members. Earlier involvement might bring different perspectives and utilize board expertise in a more creative way for a better outcome. Working with boards on their development, I am struck by members, especially on traditional boards, who expressed little sense of ownership over certain decisions. In these cases, there is a palpable sense of frustration at being kept at arm's length and having little real input, yet at the same time being expected to be accountable for the decision when it goes wrong.

The key to effective decision making often rests in how the board conducts itself, engaged or disengaged, for example. To illustrate the difference in approach, let's consider how the same scenario might play out in two very different boards: one dysfunctional and the other Governing with Purpose.

Rosemary is the CEO of a very successful charity, the key policy influencer in its field: she and her deputy are very well networked and have drawn up ambitious three-year development plans, which they now want to share with the board. Let's see what happens...

Dysfunctional board

Rosemary has some trepidation about taking her plan to the board, as they traditionally take a very hands-off approach and it's three years since they last had a strategy away day. But she's delighted when the Chair, Nancy, agrees to set another meeting to review the proposals. She presents her three-year development plan for discussion on the day, along with a staffing plan to deal with current vacancies. As she sits down, she's quietly pleased: she thinks she's covered the ground well and set out a clear and convincing case for how they can maximize the opportunities

---

[3] Stephen Covey, *The Speed of Trust*, 2006.

ahead. So, she's not prepared for what happens next: Nancy rounds on her and accuses her of trying to bounce the board into making a decision.

Instead of addressing the plan, the board focus their attention on the staff vacancies and demand to know why these haven't been dealt with already. In future, they agree that this should be a board decision, and Rosemary must supply full costings and job specs before the board will discuss the plan. They barely comment on the contents of the development plan itself.

She goes home deflated and frustrated. Six months later, she resigns.

Governing with Purpose board

Rosemary is excited about taking her plans to the board. She knows exactly when her opportunity will arrive, as regular strategy sessions are built into the board calendar – in fact, that's driven the timetable for her planning. She's worked alongside the Chair to co-design the nature and purpose of the day, and as always it will be facilitated by an external consultant to ensure a productive conversation that covers all the important areas. She and the Chair, Cathal, have agreed in advance that the purpose of the day is to seek agreement in principle and prioritize the actions/decisions required, rather than sign off on the plan immediately.

She has circulated papers in advance and as all board members have read these, her presentation can be brief and to the point. Afterwards, the session breaks into groups to delve deep into the development plan with trustees taking an active part, and the plan is quickly approved in principle with agreement around next steps. As part of the discussion, the board expresses its concern about vacancies and asks if there are any issues that require board decisions; Rosemary is able to show them with her carefully costed staffing plan that she has it under control, and the Chair, Cathal, reaffirms the CEO-delegated powers to employ staff without first seeking board approval. They leave energized and enthusiastic for the work ahead.

Same situation, very different outcomes, depending on the relationship between Chair and CEO and the preparation and purposefulness of the board. You can see how vicious and virtuous circles quickly develop: a disengaged board who are reluctant to take decisions continue to demand more information and focus on minor points, creating more frustration and disengagement, whereas an engaged, purposeful board with good processes in place find it easier to identify and choose options, building trust and energy.

Decision-making tools

Challenging assumptions is at the heart of an effective decision-making process. It is essential that assumptions are tested through rigorous questioning, and that alternatives are both presented and assessed before rushing to make decisions. The objective of a Governing with Purpose board is to prevent pre-cooked solutions as a means of truncating the discussion and landing the board with a suboptimal decision.

So far, the chapter has identified the limitations surrounding the default model of decision. The three tools outlined below offer boards more creative approaches and therefore better chances of making better decisions. These models have been adapted from work on decision making designed by the American Hospital Association in 2018.[4]

Decision sequencing

As highlighted earlier, the binary vote gives the board, Chair, or indeed CEO, little real sense of what the board really thought about the option before them. If such an approach is used too early in a deliberative process, good ideas can be discarded and there is no way to address nuances. *The first-to-five approach allows the process to identify whether support for a proposal is tepid or roasting hot or, similarly, ice cold or lukewarm.* The raising of the number of fingers

---

[4] Jamie Orlikoff, 'Seven techniques to strengthen board decision making', 2018. Available at: https://trustees.aha.org/seven-techniques-strengthen-board-decision-making [accessed 8 April 2022].

determines the level of support. This differentiation is important if the board is faced with a series of suboptimal decisions.

Supermajority

One of the challenges of a binary vote is that it can cast trustees into 'winners and losers'. It is questionable whether a mechanism of five votes to four is the best way to decide on a major change. *A change based on one vote flipping can cause great damage to board relationships and can take a long time to repair.* Hence the opportunity to introduce a supermajority, for example two-thirds and above, should be required to introduce significant and substantive change in direction, such as changing the charity's purpose. Introducing such a threshold means that the board must spend more time discussing, listening, persuading, looking at alternatives, and having an exhaustive and rigorous process before coming the decision.

Secret ballot

Whilst this may seem somewhat dramatic and could imply a lack of trust in the governance of a charity, the reality is more prosaic. Within a board there are the 'formal power' voices of the Chair and the CEO. They may be supplemented by other members of the senior leadership team. Beyond those 'formal' voices, boards often have trustees who others look up to, powerful and passionate orators who can sway undecided board members if the binary voting approach is used.

Again, this would not be a common tactic, and is only to be used in a matter of major importance or great sensitivity. It has the benefit of getting members to focus on what is important to them and reduce the likelihood of those who are strongly in favour of a proposal winning over the lukewarm purely based on their oratory. It offers a ranking approach on which the board can choose from.

Conclusion

How boards make and take decisions is central to how charities improve and develop in the widest sense. For trustees, it is probably the most tangible evidence of your impact, or not.

In more traditional boards where the options are served up to the board, and in which the board has chosen to have little to no input other than making decisions, this disempowers boards. It also fails to utilize board expertise early in the process, which according to several studies has demonstrated improved quality in the decision-making process and, by extension the decision itself.

Trustees need to reclaim a greater role in shaping the process around strategic decision making earlier if they want to be more effective. And at the same time, resist the temptation to interfere in agreed delegated decision-making mechanisms.

7 Groupthink versus dissent

Introduction

So how do a group of people come together and take decisions on something they are interested in and care about? What impinges on their thinking and decision-making processes, and how do they establish a common approach to those matters, if indeed they do?

Much of what passes for thought on this matter often emphasizes the need to be decisive and certain. These actions and traits have become fashionable in some quarters. From this perspective, reflecting and reviewing can be characterized as indecision, rather than making a choice. But in the world of board governance, thankfully, there are few situations where there is only one choice, and which require immediate action. Speed and certainty are not always synonymous with effective governance.

Either way, it is the willingness of the board to go through a process that allows for the most effective decision to emerge, rather than focusing on speed or certainty.

The debate about the speed of decision making and criticism of the quality of decisions references the need for better structures and greater clarity around processes. In some instances that critique is true. There is no doubt that some governance failings can stem from that critique. However, overdependence on a structural analysis for governance failings in turn fails to address some of the deeper questions about how the boardroom functions, or does not.

It is worth restating that a board is a group of individuals who have come together to govern an organization. Functioning as an effective governing body is a challenge in human relationships. And understanding the dynamic as to how these relationships work, and how they need to work, is a critical part of effective and good governance.

So, the interplay between each of the individuals on the board and their behaviours are the key ingredients for how the board works its way through decision making, and more generally in fulfilling their roles.

Chapter aims

This chapter will highlight behaviours that impact on decision making, focusing specifically on the dangers of groupthink. In turn, it will look at the value of dissent in decision making.

Groupthink

It is a great feeling when you first join the board of an organization, particularly one whose purpose you believe in. It seems the perfect combination: contributing to something that is important to you, whilst also being around like-minded people who share your same worldview and want to make a similar contribution. So far so good, but herein can lie the problem.

One of the biggest threats to effective governance is what is termed groupthink. It is an insidious disease; if left unchecked, it can denude board governance. It is best characterized by a culture that values loyalty to the organization. Challenge and disagreement are discouraged, and in some instances seen as a threat. It becomes a culture that encourages 'one worldview' and is suspicious of heterodox opinions. Whilst much of this is unconscious, if not challenged it can become the prevailing culture in an organization.

So, what precisely is groupthink? Yale University social psychologist Irving Janis coined the term in in his seminal 1972 work *Victims of Groupthink*. Janis theorized that based on the common desire not to upset the balance of a group of people, groups of intelligent people sometimes make the worst possible decisions based on several factors. For example, the members of a group might all have similar backgrounds that could insulate them from the opinions of outside groups.

Groupthink has been around for quite a while and there have been several case studies highlighting its negative effect. The most cited example of groupthink was the decision-making process that led to the Bay of Pigs invasion in 1961. At a high point in the Cold War, the US government planned to overthrow the new revolutionary government of Cuba led by Fidel Castro.

The US was fearful that Soviet support for Cuba, only 90 miles away, could pose a serious military threat. In this instance, President Kennedy made the decision and forced it through on the strength of his character. As a result, the rest of his senior policy team chose to back the President despite having their own private concerns about the wisdom of the action. It turned out that the Bay of Pigs was a military and propaganda disaster for the US.

And it was a disaster because none of the advisors felt able to disentangle the President's objective, namely to prevent Cuba becoming a hostile miliary base, from the process on how to achieve the optimal decision. The absence of discussing and testing what alternative options were available to achieve the objective is where groupthink took over. And the rest, as they say, is history.

And whilst, thankfully, few charities face such extreme circumstances, the impulse to unite against an external threat, to regard uncomfortable questioning as disloyal or undermining of the organization, is the same attitude that resulted in the Bay of Pigs becoming a seminal example of groupthink.

You may feel that this is an extreme example and could never imagine your board in such a position. However, the road to hell, it is said, is paved with good intentions. Becoming a member of a group, for example a book club, brings some benefits. For example, it is likely to have a set of common rules and shared views. Shared views can have the advantage of binding a group together.

The board of governance for a charity can be a similar experience. In this case, the commitment to a common cause enables trustees to interact with each other. This can help cement common cause. The downside, however, is a reluctance to challenge one another, believing erroneously that disagreement creates disharmony. And in turn, this has a negative impact on the effectiveness of the board.

No doubt you have experienced some of these behaviours in boards, as will have others. I know that I have and continue to see them acted out when observing boards. So, it is important to recognize that groupthink takes place more often than we think, and in terms of good governance, more often than we would like. And the desire to avoid conflict in a group where there is a shared purpose can have its downside in the quality of decisions the group makes.

The impact of groupthink

As Janis argues, it creates a dynamic where creativity is stifled in the interests of the group. He identified eight traits of groupthink, all of which led to flawed conclusions.[1]

1	Direct pressure
2	The illusion of invulnerability
3	The illusion of unanimity
4	Self-censorship
5	Stereotyping
6	Unquestioned belief
7	Rationalising
8	Mind guarding

Some of these traits may be familiar to you and whilst they have different emphases, they bring out the same purpose, namely, to reduce questioning and focus on consensus. This

---

[1] Irving Janis, *Victims of Groupthink*, p. 3.

is either for a genuine, if misguided, reason to minimize conflict or, more worryingly, to manipulate and maintain the dominance of leaders. Either way, they can have a profound impact on board governance.

Case study

A successful social care charity had the opportunity to merge with a bigger one and develop a key strategic partnership. On paper it looked like an ideal arrangement. It doubled the size of the organization, providing it with significant capital assets. The proposed oversight board was populated with key influencers.

A board meeting was called by one of the charities at which the other charity spoke. After a glowing presentation, the Chair, Ali, indicated that a vote should be taken to 'agree in principle' to the merger. Everyone agreed bar one of the trustees, Liam, who indicated that the process was being rushed and could not be approved at this stage as there was a lack of due diligence. He was concerned that it sounded like a takeover rather than a merger. The Chair asked him to reconsider, which he refused to do. The meeting became ugly with Liam being accused by the other trustees of trying to wreck the merger which everyone else agreed with, and that he was motivated by malice (he had previously been Chair).

The Chair called for another vote and the merger was approved. Liam resigned. Six months later, the merger collapsed. The board of the other charity cited concerns over due diligence.

In their eagerness to give their approval, the board forgot its responsibility to look after the assets of their charity and assure themselves that the action of merging could be 'stood over'. Their failure to test the risk meant that anyone who asked questions was seen as disloyal to the charity. Classic groupthink.

Of the eight traits outlined above, four traits are of particular relevance to boards in the charity sector.

Shared illusion of unanimity

A good example would be a dominant Chair who wishes to close the debate. It begins with the Chair stating that all are agreed, whilst studiously avoiding eye contact and indicating that the meeting should 'move on'. Whether it's a power play or a desire to avoid confrontation, the implication is that it is better to have a quick decision rather than one that is fought over.

Stereotyping

A variant on the above, this leads to ignoring or demeaning those who may challenge or oppose. This is where the Chair targets a 'dissenting' voice with the immortal line:

> We know you have strong views on the matter, which we have heard before, but we have a tight agenda. I would rather hear from someone whose views are less negative.

It is difficult to underestimate the damage such a response can have on the board as an entity. It can result in an increase in 'dissident' voices or a sullen withdrawal and disengagement by the targeted trustee. Either way, it has an impact on the quality of governance around the board table.

Self-censorship

The consequence of such behaviour leads to another trait, namely self-censorship. This is when those who may wish to deviate from the apparent group consensus end up self-censoring. This is on the basis that even if they had different information, the rest of the board will not want to hear it, as it might upset the consensus. It is also setting a dangerous example to others, who may adopt such a similar approach of self-censorship. As an individual trustee, this can have a corrosive effect on your confidence, as well as compromising your ability to fulfil your role.

Direct pressure

There is an expectation on those who question to conform to the dominant view. Of all these traits, it is the most dangerous to effective board governance. Those who question are seen as disloyal and are pressurized to desist.

When these traits exist in your board, one thing can be guaranteed: the ability of the board to thoroughly assess risk and evaluate policy options is inevitably limited by the overwhelming demand for loyalty and agreement. Why is this so? Well, as was highlighted in the illusion of unanimity and direct pressure traits, critical questioning and information that doesn't fit with the dominant narrative is not welcomed. This begs several questions about consequences.

1   Has the board actually arrived at the most optimal decision? After all, if you as a trustee are self-censoring or feel under pressure to conform, has not this restricted your full testing of options?
2   What impact does it place on your levels of trust in other trustees and the Chair? Does it get you to question the motives of fellow trustees who choose to remain silent?
3   Does it not bring about a more deferential board? Does that oblige you to buy into a narrative led by a dominant group that you would not want to challenge?

Some challenges

In placing such a store on loyalty, groupthink allows for the labelling of personal styles that stimulate debate, such as curious and inquiring questioning, as promoting dissent. And in that board atmosphere where there is frustration about delay and the need to move on, these challenges or disagreements can be interpreted as something else, as designed to elicit support for an alternative Chair or officer bearer, or that this person wants to get their own way.

Yet those who challenge, critically question or refuse to agree to a particular decision should not be on the receiving end of queries about their loyalty to the organization, merely because they do not agree with the majority view. Nor should challenge be equated with disloyalty. And because of the pressures that loyalty can germinate, one of the consequences of groupthink is the board not rigorously testing or challenging proposals from either the Chair or CEO, resulting in what is termed a 'rubber stamping board'.

Groupthink can become a negative force that is damaging to board governance. It has an impact on the board dynamics, where those who question are regarded as difficult, not collaborators or mavericks. Yet to be highly effective, boards need a trustee who asks the awkward question, or states 'the emperor has no clothes' – it is always a good discipline to tackle assumptions and test risk. The Chair needs to set a tone that challenges groupthink and create an environment of curious enquiry that energizes the board.

Diversity is a good challenge to groupthink; therefore, the Chair needs to cultivate new members. At the same time, the Chair needs to review the performance of board members, identify any talent gaps and seek different voices to bring to the board.

The board needs to establish a culture about how disagreement/dissent is accommodated when a decision has been agreed by a majority view. Are board members then expected to follow 'the line' despite voting against it, and in turn support the decision in public?

So, boards need to understand the insidious nature of groupthink. And whilst it is recognized that its practice in many boards is not driven by the malign intent of, for example, cults and closed institutions, where it operates in a very mind-controlling way, it does create a culture where the critical faculties of challenge are not overly encouraged, to say the least. And that ushers in a more quiescent attitude from directors, where more emphasis is placed on agreeing the decision rather than questioning it.

That view of the trustee as 'supporter' rather than 'critic' can evolve into becoming deference in how they hold the organization to account, an equally insidious position which is the antithesis of Governing with Purpose.

Deference

Whilst deference is not confined to boards who are affected by groupthink, it is certainly exacerbated by it. In the context of groupthink, deference is exhibited in two distinct areas around board governance.

Firstly, in relation to the CEO and executive team. Previous chapters have already highlighted the asymmetrical power relationship between trustees and the CEO and this does not need to be repeated here.

Suffice it to say that when the CEO is an expert in the areas of a particular problem, sometimes trustees find it difficult to test or challenge the solutions offered as they might not have the particular expertise. And if there is a culture within the board of listening to the dominant voice, it is likely to be by default.

The reality is that the CEO, and by extension the executive team, have (or should have!) a comprehensive understanding of how the organization works. This should include insights on strategic strengths and weaknesses, and expert knowledge in the field in which they operate.

They have access to extensive amounts of information, regular contact across the breadth of the charity, and free flow of actions and updates. Contrast that with board members who meet once a month for a fleeting period and have occasional interactions with the CEO outside of the board meetings.

Most of the decisions made by charities are made in meetings. This is true whether around the board table or at the desks of the CEO and executive team. This can create a situation where trustees, albeit unconsciously, can exhibit deference to the CEO and to some extent other senior management staff. This can surface in areas where the CEO is seen as an expert in a particular area, and the board is dependent upon their expertise to solve a problem or suggest a change.

Yet in that very situation trustees have given their power away. They are not there to compete on a technical level, but to assess the efficacy of proposals, evaluate the reasoning behind them and ask whether there are different options. It may be there are no better alternatives, but boards should try to go through that process. Or accept that on balance the professional opinion from the CEO is the best decision that the board can make at this time.

However, if trustees are not clear that their role is a governance and leadership one, or have the confidence to carry it out, including challenging the CEO, they will surrender much of their authority. Deference by board members does not aid good decision making.

One of the challenges related to deference is what Leigh Thompson, Professor of Dispute Resolution and Organisation at the Kellogg School of Management, terms as dominance dynamics. She defines this as one or two people dominating meetings, making it difficult for others to offer insights, especially those who are introverts.

If the dominant person is the Chair, this can make it even more difficult for diverging views to emerge. Others tend choose to feed back the opinions the Chair has expressed. So, the questioning of assumptions, always the first place to start for a board seeking to assess risk, or the presentation of alternatives that may exist in the rest of the board, do not surface.

Thompson's evidence highlights that in one six-person group, three people did 72% of the talking. And whilst that evidence was garnered from teams, and not specifically from boards, the general principle is applicable. Indeed, from my own experience of sitting on and working with boards, these ratios are familiar.

The consequence is a limited decision-making process, with status becoming the determinant factor in the contribution, rather than the contribution itself. So, people do not say what they think, but what they think the leader wants to hear. Deferring to the dominant speakers, either due to lack of confidence or fear of being targeted as disloyal or a dissenter, can create at best an empty 'echo chamber' and at worst have a corrosive impact on the principles of good governance.

Yet for effective decision making to work well, difference and different perspectives are required. If not, it means that decisions are arrived at too early, or that they are viewed from too narrow a lens. Either way, the end point can be a suboptimal decision. And even if it is not, the lack of board culture that encourages diversity of thought weakens governance.

Tip

Ask a trustee to attend your board meeting and give feedback on their observation of the meeting. Seeking that outsider view could be helpful in finding out what the behaviours in your meeting are really like.

Dissent

Yet how do boards move beyond groupthink? And how does your board prevent groupthink from taking hold in the first place?

The answer is appreciating the value of dissent for you as a trustee and for your board. *Dissent is the antithesis of groupthink and if used as both a principle, i.e. the right to disagree and be heard, and a technique, i.e. to challenge assumptions, it will improve the quality of decision making within the board.*

So, what is meant by dissent? It is said that all human progress comes from dissent, whether it was Copernicus challenging the prevailing orthodoxy of medieval times that the sun followed the Earth, or the Wright brothers proving that human flight was possible. These examples, and there are many more, highlight that an unwillingness to uncritically accept the prevailing and dominant view, and to evaluate and debate the evidence behind such views, has an enormous impact.

And following that logic through, board trustees are obliged to ensure that planned decisions are optimal and, if not, to seek the best in the prevailing circumstances. How is that to be achieved? By testing the options thoroughly via questions that 'dig deep' and allowing for airing of thoughts/ideas and views. This requires a board culture that recognizes all trustees have a different way of processing, assessing and refining decisions, and to see that as a strength not a weakness. Those who challenge the prevailing orthodoxy of the time place loyalty to an idea above loyalty to a group. In wanting to avoid groupthink, as a trustee you should do likewise, as your first loyalty is to the purpose of the charity.

Holding true to that purpose requires you to be fearless in seeking the best choices and the best decisions that strengthen and grow the charity. This entails thorough interrogation of information, seeking clarity around choices and options. It requires patience and diligence to sift through what may be a series of suboptimal choices, trying to determine the least bad. That is the stuff of leadership and governance. And it may require difficult conversations with fellow directors, some of whom may be friends and for whom you have respect.

But it cuts both ways. Fellow directors should not be constructing a moral dilemma for you and asking you to put loyalty above good governance. Whether conscious or unconscious, such pressure is not the behaviour of a governance board, but that of a friendship group.

So rather than criticizing those who wish to ask questions and are reluctant to agree until a choice is fully explored to their satisfaction, recognize that these trustees are exercising due diligence. It is that commitment to fulfilling their role that keeps the charity safe.

The effecting of a board requires awkward questions and questioning and dissenting voices, 'the Emperor has no clothes' of fable fame. That requires different perspectives. Diversity of thought is the lifeblood of Governing with Purpose. As Matthew Syed puts it in *Rebel Ideas*, 'For diversity to work its magic, judgement just be exercised'.[2]

Exercising your right to disagree during the decision-making process does not make you disloyal or a dissident; rather, you are exercising your roles and responsibilities effectively. For the same reason, failure to exercise due diligence, for the sake of maintaining friendships with other board directors, or not wanting to be regarded as part of the 'awkward squad' or a maverick, is putting one's own sensibilities first and at the expense of the organization.

The Chair has a particular role to play in setting the right tone. Governing with Purpose leaders understand that wise

---

[2] Matthew Syed, *Rebel Ideas*, 2019, p. 99.

decisions depend on the input of others and adhere to the concept of getting as many brains around the table as possible. Though such a tone should not be left solely to the Chair. As a board trustee you should push for an engaged and inclusive process on decision making and challenge Chairs who wish to dominate and offer up groupthink approaches.

It is those assets of curiosity and critical enquiry that need to dominate boardrooms, to allow for evaluation of proposals and having the space to plan better ones. The word dissent is often used in a pejorative sense, implying resistance to an idea. Boards committed to good governance will want to ensure that their decisions are optimal and, if not, the best they can be in the prevailing circumstances.

And how is that assumptions are best evaluated? By those who are unconvinced that the evidence or views presented can confirm a particular assumption. Provided the basis of those dissenting positions are based on commitment to the charity's purpose and not driven by personal motivation or self-aggrandisement, that is a demonstration of real loyalty based on wanting the best for the organization. Boards who want to Govern with Purpose will regard debate and dissent as central to improving the quality of the decision-making process.

Conclusion

So, what needs to be done? Firstly, as already indicated, boards need to be alive to the challenges posed by groupthink to the quality of governance. This requires boards to rediscover one of their most important attributes, the ability to bring a distinct perspective, expertise or lived experience, detached from the day-to-day responsibility of operational management.

Secondly, encourage curiosity and different points of view. These behaviours are central to good governance and decision making. Simply put, diversity of thought needs to trump loyalty. Trustees need to realize that one of their primary responsibilities is to have an effective decision-making process, not one that is free of disagreement or challenge.

It is fostering that mindset around and across the board table that is the key to better decision making, making it less likely that groupthink, or deference, will take root in the board. That means disagreements, dissent and diversity of thought are all attributes of good governance.

Thirdly, board trustees need to know 'why' they are on the board, and what their role is. Trustees should regard themselves as 'culture carriers' and 'super spreaders' of good governance. This means supporting and challenging colleagues to develop good behaviours such as diversity of thought, and bringing an outside eye, and conceptual depth and distance, to their governance. That is achieved through critical enquiry and curiosity being exercised by trustees. For the same reason, recognize the danger of superspreading poor behaviours such as groupthink and deference.

Fourthly, recognize that the good behaviours already referred to cannot be left to the Chair or single trustee to be the sole keeper of the flame. They need to be owned by the whole board and practised by them. And what this means is that trustees need to challenge each other regarding any drift into 'echo chambers', and ensure that there is a safe environment for the expression of disagreement and dissent.

Finally, recognize unconscious bias within and between the board, as well as by the CEO and executive team. Unconscious bias is as insidious as groupthink, and even more damaging. The practice of the senior management, as a first step, will help set the board on a firmer footing for tackling deference and groupthink, two of the most dangerous conditions that good boards can face. This can be hard for boards to deal with, but it is something that board members need to work on individually as well as in a group setting, and should be seen as an area for regular scrutiny and continuous development.

8 Strategy versus scrutiny

Introduction

As a board director, would you describe your role as more rear-view mirror, i.e. scrutiny, or more windscreen view, i.e. strategy? The question brings together the two major duties of board directors, namely their fiduciary duty, i.e. scrutiny, and their strategy duty.

The research for this book included interviews. I spoke with several board directors to get their perspective on how they would describe the two major duties outlined above; the answers were revealing, especially on scrutiny. Their description included the following:

- As a trustee my job is to hold the CEO to account.
- Seeking reassurance on what the staff are actually doing.
- Making sure that the assets of the charity are well used on the things that our purpose states.
- Keeping a close eye on the budget and what it is spent on, and if it is justifiable.
- To be able to assess the effectiveness of the performance of the charity.

These are themes that many board trustees will be familiar with. After all, the job of the board is to ensure that there are operating models in place, that they are resourced and supported, and that activity is monitored.

Chapter aims

The aim of this chapter is to explore what carrying out these duties means, analyse why trustees focus more on scrutiny than strategy, and finally to highlight the added value that trustees can bring to strategy.

What is scrutiny?

When trustees were asked to explain what scrutiny meant for them, I found that three words kept coming up and were used almost interchangeably: accountability, oversight and stewardship. According to the *Cambridge Dictionary*, scrutiny means: 'The careful and detail examination of something to get information about it', whilst stewardship is defined by *Lexico.com* as 'The job of supervising or taking care of something, such as an organization or property'.[1] *Merriam-Webster*'s definition of oversight is 'watchful and responsible care'.[2]

These words seem to encapsulate much of what the duties of a board are. Indeed, that is confirmed by looking at specific obligations on board trustees as defined by the Charity Commission.[3] The key ones are outlined below:

- Act in the best interests of the charity.
- Manage the charity's resources responsibly.
- Act with reasonable care and skill.
- Ensure that your charity is accountable.
- Comply with the charity's governing document and the law.

---

[1] Cambridge Dictionary, definition of *scrutiny*. Available at: https://dictionary.cambridge.org/dictionary/english/scrutiny. Lexico.com, Oxford University Press, definition of *stewardship*. Available at: www.lexico.com/definition/stewardship [accessed 8 April 2022].

[2] Merriam-Webster, definition of *oversight*. Available at: www.merriam-webster.com/dictionary/oversight [accessed 8 April 2022].

[3] The Charity Commission, 'Charity Commission guidance', 2019. Available at: www.gov.uk/guidance/charity-commission-guidance [accessed 8 April 2022].

These provide the framework for trustees to undertake their scrutiny and stewardship responsibilities. The challenge is to stick with the *directing not doing* mantra. So the question is, as a trustee, how to maintain scrutiny without getting sucked into operational or micro-management detail?

When carrying out your scrutiny role, realize the power of the question to open up a scrutiny discussion. Often the first reaction is to ask for more information from the CEO on a matter. Yet, of itself, asking for more information does not necessarily fulfil the scrutiny test; it merely generates more activity. Trustees need to value the power of questions more in relation to scrutiny. And as Ram Charam puts it in *Boards that Deliver*, 'how boards approach monitoring sends important signals to management. If it focuses solely on legal compliance and digging deep into minutiae, management will tend to respond with detailed reports. And if the board focuses on wide issues, management will reflect that'.[4]

Trustees, unencumbered by operational responsibilities or loyalties, can bring a detached eye. Their observations are the added value that board trustees bring to governance. Therefore, the board must not regard scrutiny as a synonym for accountability. By all means hold the CEO and indeed the executive team to account for failing to meet targets, but scrutiny is much more than that. Here are three specific examples.

Delegation

As soon as a charity has its first employee, delegated decision making starts. In a growing charity this can be a significant challenge. Boards need to let go and ensure that the CEO and rest of the executive team increase their day-to-day operational control of the performance of the charity. Many charities also have power to delegate decision making to sub-committees or senior staff. Delegation can contribute to better governance,

---

4 Ram Charam, *Boards that Deliver*, 2005, p. 139.

but the board remains collectively responsible for all decisions that are made and actions that are taken with their authority.

The role of the board is to ensure that management has clear processes and procedures on delegation. Namely, what is delegated, to whom, for what purpose and to what financial level? So, in relation to delegation what does the board need from its scrutiny? Here are some key questions.

- Is it being consistently applied?
- How is the CEO able to give such assurances?
- What is the likelihood of misuse of the system and what failsafe mechanisms are in place?

By getting the CEO or another member of the executive team to talk through how the process works, explaining who is involved and the failsafes should anything go wrong, it allows the board to do more than hold the CEO to account for the operation of the policy. *It starts with questioning whether such a policy is in the best interests of the charity.* The board needs to decide whether the answers provide sufficient reassurance. A regular report on delegation can assist with that reassurance. And at the same time it stress tests whether the process is fit for purpose.

Financial scrutiny

Scrutiny of financial planning and budgeting is usually the most challenging area of board governing. In one sense that is welcome. It demonstrates that trustees are taking their fiduciary duties seriously. Not least the added pressure of funders, especially statutory agencies, who have clear expectations on the use and the management of their funds.

And to complicate matters, charities usually have 'restricted funds' – i.e. for specific purposes, and unrestricted funds – which need no explanation. In terms of accountability as to how the money is spent, the board Treasurer, and the CEO or Director of Finance are responsible for sign-off.

Much of the day-to-day operational spend will be approved by the CEO with budget performance reported to the board or, in large charities, a finance/resources committee.

To be effective, scrutiny needs to focus on the trends, not the arithmetic. Again, the quality of the questions is key to effective scrutiny.

As this is a review of what has happened, the scrutiny questions need to be about identifying trends. So the question asked to the CEO should be: *is there anything about the underspend/overspend that is surprising?* That is a more significant governance question than why are you under/overspent? These questions provide a basis to determine whether the board requires corrective action to be taken in the next quarter and indeed for the rest of the year. The answer determines what happens next.

There is a real danger that trustees get sucked into questioning operational levels of spend that have little significance to the wider financial outturn. As a trustee, whilst you may feel virtuous identifying an 'unnecessary spend', it is ineffective if the wider issue is a huge shortfall. Remember that the purpose behind the scrutiny of the budget process is to test whether the financial resources of the charity can match existing expenditure and, if not, what needs to be done. That should lead to questions such as:

- *Is the actual expenditure aligned with the mission/purpose of the charity?*
- *Can better outcomes be met by concentrating on fewer and more specific objectives?*

These questions ensure that the board and trustees are holding the CEO to account, exercising leadership and governance rather than behaving like operational managers checking individual lines on a budget. It needs to be recognized that this might be the way that trustees learn more about the financial position. However, the Chair and CEO need to suggest more effective ways in which to learn.

Trustworthiness is at the heart of any scrutiny process. Onora O'Neill, an eminent philosopher, is cited by David Spiegelhalter as saying that *people do not seek to be trusted, since that is granted by others, but to demonstrate the trustworthiness of their work.* O'Neill offers a specific checklist of what trustworthiness requires: honesty, reliability and competence. This is of particular importance around information. This is what David Spiegelhalter calls 'being transparent, not just dumping data, but making it accessible, intelligible, and useable'.[5]

So, it is up to the CEO or the executive team to demonstrate their bona fides in providing information that aids trustees. Where there is a reluctance to give full disclosure and transparency, it creates an impression that key facts are being hidden. If not dealt with, a climate of mutual suspicion emerges with trustees accusing senior management of withholding information and senior management accusing trustees of 'trying to catch them out'.

Such a climate does little to engender trust, and for trustees can be a lose–lose situation. Getting into a scrap over detail is not where you should be. Instead, focusing on the high-level measurement and assessment of financial performance is where trustees should concentrate.

Scrutinizing the board

Much of this chapter has concentrated on how boards carry out their scrutiny role in relation to policy, process, finances and operational performance. It has dwelt on the potential tensions between the board and senior staff. And whilst holding the CEO and executive team to account is the most recognized component of the role, scrutiny should not stop there.

There is little discussion about how trustees scrutinize their own performance and hold each other to account. Yet for a Governing with Purpose board, such principles are critical to good governance. Trustees should realize they have a key role to set the tone and hold each other to account, and should not rely on the Chair alone.

It is vital that poor behaviour by individual trustees is challenged – whether this is not being prepared for meetings or acting contrary to the ethos of the charity or conflicts of

---

[5] David Spiegelhalter, The Art of Statistics, 2019, p. 368.

interest. So whether this is rudeness to the CEO or other board trustees, impatience with different thought processes of trustees, or a Chair trying to 'railroad' the board to a decision, all these poor behaviours should be questioned, challenged and tackled. Why? Simply put, for the quality of governance and the benefit of the whole board.

Risk

Every charity faces a range of risks – strategic, financial, operational, compliance and more. Some of these risks may be identifiable, whilst others could be unknown and unanticipated. The failure to effectively manage any of these risks can impact on reputation, and perhaps even the ability to continue operating. Not all risks are equal, and the board needs to focus first on the risks that pose an existential threat to the viability of the charity and work down from there.

Scrutiny is not to prove there are no risks, but rather to identify them, assess the level of threat, and either resolve through action or have a backup plan. As well as assessing risks to the charity, trustees should also be testing the appetite for risk between the board and the executive team. Why is this important? Well, as we will go on to discuss in the section on strategy, it helps to sense check where everyone is in terms of development and strategy planning.

Tip

Using scenario planning models at strategy days provides a safe space to discuss levels of risk in relation to specific examples.

Risks change and adapt. Therefore, as a best practice board, it should formally assess the inventory of risks to be monitored on an annual basis. This does not mean that all risks need to be mitigated, but all risks should be identified and risk mitigation should be prioritized.

Strategy

Unlike scrutiny where the role of the board and trustees is pretty clear, roles in relation to strategy are less so. Conversations with trustees about strategy often reveal frustration and confusion about how they should exercise their role.

Whilst boards are ultimately responsible for the strategic direction of their charities, common practice often places the design of strategy in the hands of the CEO and the executive team. As a result, some boards are nothing more than a 'rubber stamp' of the CEO's strategic thinking, whilst others, trying to get more involved in strategic thinking and shaping direction, face resistance from the CEO and executive team.

Neither approach makes sense nor allows trustees to truly add value. Yet as this book is entitled *Governing with Purpose*, it is precisely in this area that boards and, in particular, you as an individual trustee have much to offer and be more involved. Such an approach provides an opportunity to share expertise and where the perspective of trustee can bring something fresh to shaping strategy and not just critiquing the finished article.

This section will challenge the traditional positioning of trustees' roles in relation to strategy, arguing that they should have a much greater role in shaping and designing it.

What is meant by strategy?

Perhaps the best place to start is a definition. The Collins Dictionary defines strategy as follows: 'A strategy is a general plan, or a set of plans intended to achieve something, especially over a long period'.[6]

The dictionary definition highlights the dilemmas that boards can face. As a reader, no doubt you are already asking what is a 'plan', how is it achieved and defined, and what is meant by a 'long period'? This clearly shows that strategy has many

---

[6] Collins Dictionary, definition of *strategy*. Available at: www.collinsdictionary.com/dictionary/english/strategy [accessed 8 April 2022].

possible meanings and therefore each board must decide what it means to them.

The lack of a universally accepted, up-to-date meaning for strategy often results in boards sticking to the most traditional concepts – vision, mission and values. Thus, little time is dedicated to thinking about what they might be able to achieve if they took the time to explore what strategic thinking means to them.

So, what should the board's role be vis-à-vis strategy? Again, there are many variations – stretching from standoff oversight to co-design of strategy with the executive team and CEO. Inevitably, the board's involvement in strategy will depend on the context or environment the charity works in. It will also be impacted by the culture of the board: whether it is hands-off or interventionist.

How should boards engage in strategy?

Leading thinkers and researchers have highlighted several ways in which boards can better engage in strategy. Three of the most relevant to the charity sector will be discussed next.

Strategy as planning

In this perspective, strategy serves to establish the organizational vision/mission/values and purpose. It helps define the long-term objectives, action programmes and resource allocation priorities. It is the traditional approach to strategy. This definition gave birth to the notion of 'strategic planning', which has become an established practice, though it is heavily criticized by management thought leaders such as Henry Mintzberg in his book *The Rise and Fall of Strategic Planning*.

Strategy as a focused response to overcome a key challenge

In his book, *Good Strategy/Bad Strategy*, Richard Rumelt states that strategy 'consists of diagnosing the nature of the key challenges, developing an overall approach to overcome the obstacles and designing a set of coordinated actions to accomplish the defined approach'.[7] The challenge may come from the risks and opportunities in the economic and business environment, or it may arise from the competitive landscape.

It can even stem from internal issues such as an organizational structure that is no longer fit for purpose. Identifying, assessing and managing risks and opportunities will lead to a focused approach and coordinated actions that are the heart of this definition of strategy. These are often led by the CEO who either reports the analysis to the board with recommended actions or acts in response to the board seeking a risk assessment on the changed environment. This example is of particular relevance to the charity sector.

Strategy as identifying and reinforcing core competencies

In this situation, strategy is a vehicle for achieving long-term sustainable competitive advantage. A specific example would be a social care agency that provides services across a wide spectrum of care conditions, but building on the core competencies of specialist staff to enable expansion and growth.

In the first instance, boards need to decide which is their preferred engagement strategy. This is by no means a static decision, as one view may be more relevant to the short term, and others to longer-term sustainability. So determining how early the board want to get involved, and how best to use the respective expertise of trustees and the CEO/executive is important. Many disagreements within boards and between boards and the CEO can be avoided by having a discussion at the start of any strategy process.

This might be done by asking each trustee to assign points to each of the definitions of strategy and then tallying the results to uncover the differences of view and determine which one(s) rank highest among all board members. Such a process is part

7 Richard Rumelt, *Good Strategy/Bad Strategy*, 2017, p. 41.

of intent-based leadership, developed by David Marquet.[8] It provides an opportunity to air different perspectives and build a coordinated view among the board.

Determine your board's role

Some argue that strategy can only be achieved by a hands-on individual with deep organizational knowledge, i.e. the CEO. This is best associated with a traditional view of the CEO/board relationship. However, even this view agrees that the board should challenge the CEO's strategic thinking if only to convince themselves of the CEO's ability. So even the most traditional/remote boards still have a role to fulfil in relation to strategy. Of course, board culture as well as existing board custom and practice will determine how their strategic muscle is used.

There are three possible roles that a board might decide to adopt in relation to strategy development: support, oversight and co-design.

Support

In this role, the board acts largely as a support for management, and seeks the strategy from the CEO/executive team. Not being directly involved gives objectivity and authority, and the board's stamp of approval can bring credibility to major strategic shifts as well as minor ones.

In times of crisis, a supportive board can be the key to success. In the same way that boards can rank and map their definitions of strategy across options, they can do the same for weighting and mapping the roles they seek to play – oversight, supervisory, design.

For example, a board cannot decide to act just in a supportive role unless it is convinced of the quality and performance of what the CEO and executive team produces. On the other

---

[8] See Intent-Based Leadership International. Available at: https://intentbasedleadership.com/ [accessed 8 April 2022].

hand, it might want to co-create the strategy with the executive team. What counts is that the board decide their role, which determines their level of involvement.

Oversight

The role of the board is to monitor the performance of the CEO and the executive team. The board is there to ensure the performance of the charity. This oversight includes everything – strategy development, design and implementation. It requires the board to have a systematic view, attention to detail, and an understanding of consistency and control. Therefore, trustees need to assess for risks, strategic inconsistencies and flaws. Developing these oversight skills is thus a prerequisite for board supervision of strategy and that means deciding what is truly important and focusing action and resources on that objective, as Richard Rumelt recommends.[9]

Co-design

From a Governing with Purpose perspective, this is the preferred option in relation to trustee and board empowerment. In this approach, trustees' expertise and critical appraisal skills are used from the beginning of the strategy process. Successful co-design will typically access both the internal information held among the executive team as well as experience gathered from the board to produce a long-term perspective with more options and flexibility than typically comes from managerial focus alone.

Such an approach allows trustees to bring their expertise to shape the process at an early stage, enhancing the creativity available. This should be followed up by a strategy blueprint, which is a vehicle to build consensus on the organization's strategic direction.

Once the strategy has been agreed, how it is monitored to assess impact on performance and goals is essential. Enabling clarity on the strategic outcomes will produce two benefits. Firstly, the process will be trusted as it has been shaped by the board

---

[9] Richard Rumelt, *Good Strategy/Bad Strategy*, 2017, p. 90.

trustees themselves, and secondly, CEOs have a workable plan that has been agreed by the board.

Challenges boards face

Any book on board governance will include the advice that the board needs to spend time on strategy. Yet even raising the issue can unearth a frustration felt by many boards. Trustees will seek guarantees for a strategy that will continue to grow the organization and maintain financial stability. On the other hand, CEOs get frustrated by the board revisiting the question, even after answers have been given, hoping for a better one. So, making it a better experience for all is critical to better governance and better strategy.

Why is it that board strategy development can cause such angst? Quite simply, how it is discussed goes much of the way to cause this angst. There are several bad practices that boards engage in which lessen the likelihood of a positive experience; improving their practice would provide a basis for a reset. Two particular examples are:

1   Firstly, having a discussion about strategy at the end of a long board meeting. The rationale for this practice is that everyone is already there, and it avoids scheduling another meeting for busy people. *Such an approach is a recipe for disaster and is likely to result in poor decisions.*
2   Secondly, the absence of thought and planning on how the session will operate before any strategy discussion. Adopting a regular board meeting approach will not allow the development of critical thoughts, fresh perspectives and breaking out of the known, all of which are essential. Without such an approach, the strategy is likely to be of limited value.

Making strategy work

Strategy goes to the heart of the purpose and mission of the charity. It asks, 'are we there yet and, if not, what do we do to get there?' So, in making strategy work for trustees and boards there are five key elements.

- Set aside enough thinking and discussion time. After all, a strategy will cover a lifespan of up to five years, and that requires a different process.
- Give real thought to how the conversation takes place. A structured way in a different environment with an external facilitator allows trustees to take different perspectives and look at themes and ideas beyond their own interests and focus on the future for the charity.
- The conversation on strategy should result in clarity specifics on priorities and succinctness in how it is described. These provide a strong basis on which the board can measure performance.
- A climate where as trustees you all feel safe to question and challenge each other and test the efficacy of the options is crucial. It brings together the expertise and experiences of both the executive team and trustees, allowing for a better strategy.
- The strategy needs to be rebranded as a living document that guides the direction of the charity. *Thus, its place is on the board table and not in the filing cabinet.* It is critical to have a regular review of progress, testing the relevance of the priorities and adjusting them as required.

Tip

Use the strategy document to initiate discussions at board meetings on direction. This enables the strategy to be a living and relevant document.

Conclusion

Much of the core work of charity trustees is contained in this chapter. It is this work, the scrutiny role and the strategy role, that can be construed as the 'bread and butter' of governance. And as was highlighted, the tendency for trustees is to align towards scrutiny as it is more tangible, where effort and effect are easily measurable. However, as was also highlighted in the chapter, the temptation to get sucked into pursuing detail, seeking more and more information, takes trustees and the board away from their leadership and governance role.

After all, scrutiny is about assessing the past, and indeed learning lessons from it, but the past cannot be changed. So, in terms of where power and impact lie, it is in the present and the future. Therefore, the board should endeavour to get more involved in shaping the strategic direction of the charity at the beginning of the process, rather than becoming 'editors and scrutineers' at the end of the process. This brings the board to governance and leadership – which is where it should be – and that is Governing with Purpose.

Part 4

Re-imagining purpose

9 Governance as leadership

Introduction

The final section of the book is entitled 'Re-imagining purpose'. The next three chapters are both an exhortation to trustees to appreciate their value and their power and to realize it through specific areas and examples. For that to happen, trustees need to reposition around the terms governance and leadership. That means seeing themselves through a new prism, rather than a narrow focus of their responsibilities in relation to the binary separation of roles between the board and the CEO/executive team. That new prism is Governing with Purpose.

As I have attempted to convey throughout this book, it is the experiences, expertise and absence of involvement in the day to day that gives trustees their distinctive view. Governance of a charity is not just about holding the CEO and the executive team to account, important though that is. It includes bringing energy and dynamism to drive the charity forward. It is also about ensuring the ethos and purpose are not just words, but are put into practice, across the board and the rest of the charity.

That means the board initiating discussion about how the charity, and in particular the board, understand the ethos and purpose and use it as a framework for scrutiny and strategy development. As James Nathan Miller put it: 'There is no such thing as a worthless conversation, provided you know what to listen for. And questions are the breath of life for a conversation.'

This is where the real benefit for both the charity and the individual takes place, when trustees appreciate that their role is not either scrutiny or strategy, but that governance as leadership is their primary role, of which scrutiny or strategy, for example, are tools to help them carry out their role. That is not to dismiss the value of both, but they place trustees in a reactive role, overseeing the actions of others, when they need to be to directing more and monitoring less. This is especially true in the current unpredictable and uncertain environment where charities face a series of interrelated challenges:

- increased regulation post COVID-19;
- the ever-growing threat of cybersecurity breaches;
- the 'great resignation phenomenon' resulting in a competitive labour market;
- adjusting to hybrid working.

These are new challenges on top of existing ones. Many of these themes require different responses which need to come from fresh thinking and different perspectives. And that is where trustees have a distinctive contribution to make to enable the charity to navigate through these challenges and create a sustainable future. For that to happen, boards and their trustees need to think differently and act proactively.

Chapter aims

The aim of this chapter is to introduce the concept of governance as leadership. It will highlight how the relationship between the board and CEO/executive team can be recast. The chapter will also identify how this will improve board effectiveness and empower trustees to realize their value.

The need for change

Chapter 8 already outlined how boards can become engaged in the wider themes of strategy and indicated some best practice approaches to making this work. One of the key areas for trustees and boards to demonstrate governance as leadership is through a greater engagement in policy formulation than hitherto.

Historically, it has been left to the CEO and the executive team to devise policy, which the board scrutinize and approve. And whilst the CEO/executive team may have a more immediate grasp of the external policy environment as well as the need for internal policies, it does not mean that the role of the board should be solely one of critiquing and approving.

At the same time, there has been a general reluctance for the board to get involved in policy formulation for several reasons. Some boards see this a 'power' reserved to the CEO and executive team and have no appetite to get involved. For others, it is a concern about getting sucked into areas where they feel they have little knowledge. And among the executive team, there can be concern about the value that trustees will bring, and a fear of confusion if the process is not clear.

Why is this the case? Simply put, policy formulation, according to Bob Garratt, is the least understood component of a board director's role. He identifies four components of policy formulation: purpose, vision and values, emotional climate and culture. Garratt argues that these 'soft words and themes' shape the way in which the charity operates; get buy-in from staff around the strategy; and at the same times create a 'safe organization' which encourages feedback and uncomfortable truths that all good organizations need to know and need to hear.

Yet all governance needs feedback. There are times when uncomfortable truths need to be stated and heard, especially when the CEO and executive team are too close to issues and not taking a wide enough view. One place where directors can make an important contribution is in relation to the ethos and purpose of the charity. For example, testing the ethos is not just words and there needs to be alignment between what the organization says it stands for and how it puts that into practice. The ethos – how the charity carries out its purpose – is of critical importance. It is the charity's reason for existing and provides the basis for attracting funding, staff and volunteers.

It is not enough for that to be left to staff and is a core governance responsibility. That means the board initiating discussion about how the charity, and in particular the board, understand the ethos and purpose and use it as a framework for scrutiny and strategy development.

Most importantly, it is these words and the culture that they imbue that is the glue that binds the charity together. *The job of the board is to ensure that when times get tough, the purpose, values and culture are not cast aside because they cannot be afforded.* It is precisely when times are tough that the culture will play a critical role.

And in the context of policy formulation, it is for boards to decide the extent of their involvement. At the very least that should ensure that the four components referred to above are the basis for any policy formulation being drawn up for the board. After all, many boards contain trustees who work in other charities and have expertise in public policy. And whilst that understanding of the external environment can be of value to the board, the culture of how the board and trustees operate is critical to good governance.

Trustees are in an ideal place to bring dynamism to drive the organization to perform to its purpose. That will sometimes require energizing the CEO and executive team and even board trustees to think bigger and better. This is where the real benefit for both the organization and the individual is found.

The traditional division of labour between board and CEO is no longer sufficient. It also restricts trustees from bringing their outside and sometimes lived experience to the key areas that determine the effectiveness of a charity – *clarity of purpose, shared culture, clear policies and strategic direction need to be regarded as shared agendas between the board and the CEO.*

Trustees should be better at recognizing both their role and their expertise in these key areas and want to be in at the beginning of shaping policy and strategy. Their absence from the day-to-day management allows for reflection and a sense of perspective. More importantly, that involves seeing beyond their functional roles. This means reappraising the balance of roles between trustees and CEO to one of governance and leadership.

Governance as leadership

For trustees, governance as leadership should be regarded as the 'day job'. By bringing together the leadership expertise of the board and CEO/executive team, and through the use of generative work and thinking (which will be explored in the next section), it improves the likelihood of better decision making, and flowing from that, better governance. It also explicitly places trustees in a leadership role.

The principle of governance as leadership was first popularized by Chait et al.[1] *It depicts a model of fiduciary and strategy duties as a responsibility of the whole board, and not separated by the binary roles of trustees.* It is the notion of the whole board owning the actions and decisions – meaning it is more than the sum of its parts. And it is what is the key to what Chait et al. termed 'generative thinking'.

When first defined by the authors, they described it as a triangular relationship of fiduciary and strategy on either side of the triangle underpinned by generative working. I have used the design as inspiration for how governance as leadership can be best described in a Governing with Purpose board.

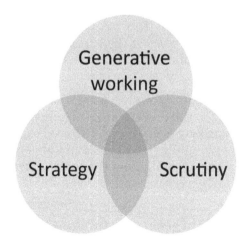

Figure 9.1: *Governance Venn diagram*

---

[1] Richard P. Chait et al., *Governance as Leadership*, 2005, p. 6.

The interconnection between the circles and where they intersect is where a Governing with Purpose board is best placed to ensure that governance as leadership is the primary role of the board collectively and trustees individually. The more that trustees are operating in the centre of the diagram, the more effective they are likely to be.

Governance as leadership provides a step change in the way in which trustees see their roles, both in terms of thinking and acting as leaders as well as feeling empowered.

Generative thinking

Generative thinking changes the dynamic in a board by recognizing that the policy development and strategic direction guiding an organization cannot be limited to separately hermetically sealed tanks of the respective responsibilities of the CEO/executive team and board trustees. Instead, it recognizes the reality of role blur and regards that as an opportunity for the CEO/executive team, combined with the expertise of the trustees to play to their strengths.

Through a co-design approach to strategy and policy formulation, it creates the opportunities for better ideas – based on the brains around the table concept. This has the advantage of enabling trustees to become involved at the beginning of the process. It addresses their frustration about being at the end of the process, limited to 'editing' policy.

Similarly, because both executives and trustees are represented at the beginning of the process, accountability and ownership is shared, thus making decisions more stickable. Also, in terms of scrutiny, accountability and ownership are shared. Hence, Figure 9.1 is a circle – it signifies the interconnectedness and virtuous circle of governance as leadership.

What is the value of generative thinking?

Generative thinking provides an awareness of what knowledge, information and data mean. It recognises that is 'owned' by the board, and at the same time sharing with both the CEO team and trustees allows for integration and co-designed decision making and strategic direction.

Some challenges

But this means facing up to some uncomfortable truths. In most charities, CEOs and the executive team are presumed to be the repository that generates the thinking and ideas for the organization and the board. And as the policy and regulatory environment becomes more complex, the board increasingly relies on the professional expertise of the executive team, which can have the effect of displacing the trustee leadership role.

So why does this happen? Most boards are on the outside looking in, as everyone else is participating in generative work. And whilst some boards do generative work some of the time, and a few board members may do so, for example when on working groups, most boards are not organized and equipped to do generative work.

This can lead to boards adopting a managerial version of governance. Instead of identifying problems and highlighting issues, from a board perspective most boards deal with the problems/issues that management and the CEO present to them. This implies that boards do not contribute, let alone lead the generative work that is critical for governance. Thus, boards can be deprived of the insights and perspectives of individuals who are charged to see beyond the immediate, restricting the vision of the charity. Boards become bystanders.

Whilst this does not apply to all boards, even in boards where there is discussion and debate, inevitably this is restricted to the priorities or focus of management. There will be times when board members' exhortations to 'think outside the box' will be heard, essentially a plea to reframe the issue. Yet unless the Chair is open to such a reframe, it can often be dismissed as a demand from a disruptive or maverick trustee who is holding up the business of the meeting.

What happens next is the board modifies on the margins, and executive team solutions to what they see as the charity's problems are ratified by the board. And whilst they may be solutions, they come from a narrow perspective, whereas a wider board purview might have produced longer-term and more comprehensive change.

However, the board will never know this as it has given up a chance to govern in favour of slipping into an assessment role, testing the efficacy of executive team plans/policy. Thus, the ultimate power of the board has not been used, and in turn it has exercised little influence on the CEO/executive team.

Now it may be that effective board scrutiny confirms the robustness of the policy designed by the executive team, but it comes from their 'known' world. Yet many boards in the charity sector will be inhabited by persons familiar with the external policy environment, either through their leadership position within another charity, or as advocates for change in public policy.

There are other examples that are equally suboptimal to boards exercising governance and leadership. In contrast to the scenario outlined above, where the board surrenders their power, there is an equally destructive approach which is best described as governance by default. In this situation, no generative thinking, far less generative work, takes place.

The vacuum is filled by the CEO and executive team who design strategies, devise business plans, develop campaigns and advocate on behalf of the charity. Essentially, 'mission creep' by the executive team into the areas for which the board has both a role and a responsibility. And whilst this mission creep may sometimes, by pure luck, reposition the charity successfully, it is equally likely to be damaging. Either way, it is an abdication of leadership.

The above highlights what happens when the organizational leaders in charity, namely the CEO/executive team and the board, do not share or plan their generative thinking. This is not to suggest that ideas from staff should be suppressed, but rather to plan and develop a harmony from discordant and differing voices if possible.

The reasons for adopting generative thinking are complex and variable. Some of them stem from the changing nature and professionalization of the CEO position within the charity sector. *As charities have become larger and more complex, and in turn working in an increasingly regulated framework, the nature of the CEO role has changed.* Many are now responsible for big staff teams, managing complex and differentiated services commissioned from public agencies. They are often expected to play the role on government working parties and regularly engage with local decision makers on health and social care.

This has brought an assumption by some boards that CEOs, aided by their executive team, are presumed to be the sole repository that generates the thinking for the charity and the board. And as the policy and regulatory environment becomes more complex, the board relies more on the professional expertise of the executive team. This can have the effect of displacing a key trustee leadership role, surrendering and diminishing power as the leaders and governors of the charity.

It is further complicated by the actual status of the CEO in relation to board governance. In charities, especially those that are social care organizations, the CEO is seen as a servant of the board. Their job is to offer policy and services priorities and give advice to the board. They attend the board, but are not of the board. It can result in both frustration from the CEO that they cannot influence directly, yet at the same time the board is not using the CEO to the best effect.

Whilst neither party is satisfied, it can be expressed by the board that the CEO is seen as the voice and the face of the board. As a result, there can be pressure on the Chair for trustees to reclaim territory from the CEO on behalf of the board.

The reality for many CEOs is that their control of the knowledge of the organization, through the day-to-day management and a performance dashboard, gives them an unrivalled understanding of what is happening. In addition, they can network with other CEOs. They can be incredibly powerful, and power is both soft and hard.

This can result in a breakdown of respect for the board by the CEO, and is often expressed in the term 'get something through the board'. When this is overheard in meetings with senior staff, it creates the impression that subterfuge is required to engineer the CEO's agenda to get board approval. This can be the case where a strong and experienced CEO is working with what they perceive to be a board that is not up to 'speed'. This then creates an impression that the board is a brake on progress and hindering the organization, leading the CEO to be dismissive of the value of the board, and describing the regular board meetings as a distracting piece of theatre.

For some CEOs it is a question of putting up with the board and finding a different way to achieve the objective. Such behaviours can result in sullen resentment at best from both sides, and a toxic relationship at worst. These have long-term effects upon board dynamics. It is important that the CEO sets clear expectations of what they want from the board and an understanding of how they will work together. To build the relationship, it should be the CEO that reaches out to board members to explain how they work and what their priorities are. This is especially important if this is a new board membership or if the CEO is new to the organization.

Facing the challenges

It is tempting then to say that if what Chait et al. term generative thinking is central to governing, why not give all the generative work to boards? However, if boards do all the generative work, they move from bystanders to implementers. Boards imposing their views on CEOs and the executive team are unlikely to be acceptable for long. The reality is that most boards recognize that staff, especially the CEO, have a pivotal role in generative work, and because of their wider roles and networks are well positioned to do the work.

This can sometimes lead to tensions with the board. CEOs may have more effective networks that trump those of the board and bypass the board to engage with key decision makers. This can lead to accusations that the CEO is supplanting the role of the board and Chair in advocating and promoting the charity.

Yet at the same time, in turn this can result in a situation where the CEO feels that the board see their role in a very narrow confine of holding the CEO to account, focusing on the detail, yet not addressing wider strategic perspectives or addressing their own performance on engagement and participation.

Getting board members to focus on their core functioning of governing requires a step change in thinking. Not only does it have the capacity to improve the quality of governance, but also offers boards a way to see the value they add and for individuals to recognize their own contribution.

Why is this the case? Most boards in connection to policy and strategy are on the outside looking in, seeing their role as solely to critique work – whilst everyone else, i.e. the CEO and executive team, is participating in generative work. Others have created an environment of 'separation of powers' akin to the 'officers propose, members dispose' traditional notion of local government decision making.

However, there is a different way to approach this. From the beginning the board and executive need to put all the challenges from their distinct positions and perspectives together. This provides the basis on which to determine, for example, whether new policies are required or when the current strategy can deliver on the charity purpose. By adopting this approach of governance as leadership, the generative work issues highlighted above are not the preserve of a group, particularly the CEO/executive, but a shared endeavour. This enables the charity to avail of the insights and expertise of individuals who are charged to see beyond the immediate and ensure long-term strategy and policy to create a sustainable organization.

The benefits of governance as leadership

The governance as leadership approach regards generative thinking as a shared endeavour. It goes a significant way to rebalance the relationships between the board and the CEO/executive team. It also assists in managing the boundaries between the Chair and CEO. This has the added advantage of preventing micro-managing and micro-governing. It also means that in relation to promoting and advocating on behalf of the charity, designing a clear strategy and clarifying the roles of the key players, it is likely to be much more effective. It allows for the right skills to be in the right place, and with the right messages for external decision makers.

Such an approach avoids a tussle between the board and the CEO as to who should engage with key stakeholders and decision makers. It also has the advantage of recognizing the respective skills of the board and the CEO, which combined with their own circles of influence are more likely to be effective together.

In relation to policy formulation, such an approach can be successful when the board is clear about where and when it wants to get involved. And whilst more involvement often results in better outcomes, it may be that the board does not want to get involved on a particular occasion. As ever, clear and early communication is important.

This can be the case where a strong and experienced CEO is working with what is perceived as a board that is not up to speed, in the way that the CEO thinks they need to be. It has the benefit of delineating the position of the board and avoids the impression that the board is a brake on progress.

Generative thinking and the board repositioning themselves as governors and leaders goes a long way to tackle what can sometimes be a zero-sum game between boards and CEOs. This produces classic behaviours whereby for some CEOs it is a question of putting up with the board and finding a separate way to achieve the objective, whether by bypassing the board or persuading a trustee to back them. Or the board seeing their sole role as to 'mark the homework' of the CEO.

Without ascribing magical properties to generative thinking, it means the areas where board trustees have chosen not to become involved, or conversely expect to have a lead role, do not become contested arenas. Suddenly, there is sufficient space and responsibilities for everyone to perform to the best they can be.

Conclusion

It is precisely for these reasons that reframing the governance and leadership of boards as the generative approach is, as Chait et al. contend, the best model for governing a charity. It means the dynamic between the well-connected professional CEO and executive team with a 24/7 knowledge of the organization and a board of trustees does not need to be a zero-sum game of winners and losers.

A co-design approach to strategy and policy formulation sums up the generative approach. For board trustees, this is such an important space for them to be, and it should not be solely colonized by the CEO and executive team.

Trustees have a responsibility to act in the best interests of the charity; it is important that their understanding of the outside world is brought to bear in shaping how the charity performs, and how it is held to its values and purpose. Such an approach keeps the CEO/executive team on their toes, enables them to benefit from the added value of that lay leadership role. It creates the space for a more rounded approach to what governing and leadership is about.

So, moving beyond the fiduciary and strategy roles, trustees should become engaged in areas where they can add value, not just in their critiquing of positions, but in their policy creativity. After all, as previously highlighted, many boards have trustees with a wealth of experience from operating at a strategic and governance level in the charity sector and beyond. So on the principle that the more brains around the table the better the solutions, trustees need to be involved at the beginning of the strategy and policy formulation development.

10 Board as ambassador and influencer

Introduction

Much of the commentary and instruction on trustee responsibilities overemphasizes strategy and scrutiny, often at the expense of their advocacy, influencing and ambassadorial roles. These roles are often forgotten about by commentators and some boards. And if not forgotten by all, certainly underutilized. Yet trustees acting as advocates or ambassadors is a demonstration of their leadership. Filling that representational space is as valuable a contribution as fulfilling scrutiny and strategy roles.

As the sector operates in a competitive market, with many charities chasing a finite amount of public and other funding, the need to raise profile and demonstrate tangible impacts from that funding continues to increase.

Chapter aims

The aim of this chapter is to outline the importance of trustees reclaiming their advocacy, influencing and ambassadorial roles. It will highlight the value to the charity that such roles can bring. It will also identify specific ways in which boards and trustees can perform these roles.

The need for change

The sector varies widely in how trustees undertake these roles, if at all. Historically, many trustees have been ambivalent about being too visible in advocating for the charity. Some would see that as the CEO role, and sometimes that of the Chair, but not theirs. And some CEOs have been reluctant to relinquish what they see as influence and 'their domain' to the board, and by extension, the Chair.

That is not to say that boards and trustees do not advocate for their cause and wider sectoral themes, because they do. The challenge is that much of that advocacy is often in reaction to an external threat or rather as part of a planned-out strategy. So there are a number of reasons why boards need to more proactive.

Firstly, the sector faces increased regulatory conditions and greater government oversight.

Secondly, the pressure to fundraise, both to replace shortfalls in government funding, and grow the unrestricted element of funds to reduce dependency on statutory funding, is enormous.

Thirdly, recent high-profile cases surrounding misuse of funds by a small number of charities, concerns about the questionable tactics of 'chuggers' and reports of six-figure salaries for CEOs have impacted upon public trust and confidence in what their donations are used for. And whilst these cases are unusual, these are unwelcome distractions.

So, it is hard to understate the pressure that many charities are under. Thus, it is even more important that advocacy and influencing become strategic activities and trustees realize how they can play a critical role in how their own charity is perceived and, by extension, the sector. Let us address each in turn.

Advocacy

According to *Lexico.com*, advocacy is 'public support for or recommendation of a particular cause or policy'.[1]

There are a number of reasons why boards and trustees need to get involved in advocacy for their charities. It is a powerful way to leverage the important work that your charity does. Being an advocate is directly connected to each trustee's fundamental responsibility to champion their charity's work and purpose.

First and foremost, many trustees join a charity board because they either have some direct knowledge of the area or work in a similar field. Others are 'supporters' of a particular organization/ sector, often because of a personal experience. That supporter/ personal commitment to a particular organization can bring an added dimension.

So, what added value can trustees bring in terms of advocacy?

An obvious starting point is for trustees to speak to those in their own business and professional circles about what their charity does. Boards often have influential community actors who are connected to others. This provides opportunities to strengthen connections, establish networks and develop advocates.

Some charities have been founded by those who have a lived or family experience of the condition that the charity works with. This is particularly true in the social care arena. These trustees can often tell powerful stories about how the charity has impacted positively on their lives. This is a safe way for trustees to develop their advocacy role, both for the individual charity and for more generally specific conditions.

Case study

A disability charity had its AGM at the height of the COVID-19 pandemic. Because it went online it got a bigger attendance of members and national politicians than usual.

---

[1] Lexico.com, Oxford University Press, definition of *advocacy*. Available at: www.lexico.com/definition/advocacy [accessed 8 April 2022].

The Chair highlighted a large representation from members seeking medical exemptions from mask wearing due to specific medical conditions. The charity circulated a proposed mock-up of an exemption notice. Weeks later they were asked by the Scottish government to design, lead and manage exemption badges and promotional material for the whole of Scotland.

Advocacy by boards can be either for their own charity or the wider sector. For example, legislative changes that improve rights and entitlements of all or a local company agreeing to sponsor a local charity are both examples of successful advocacy.

Board advocacy can also help in raising community awareness and understanding of sensitive matters. The advocacy and ambassadorial work of board trustees of HIV/AIDS charities did a lot to change public perceptions and shape policy changes due to their speaking up and speaking out.

And advocacy by the sector has had many successes. Legislative changes, enhanced awareness about conditions and improved services in many areas all attest to the effectiveness of advocacy, which benefitted many. A good example would be the deaf community's successful campaign for British Sign Language to be recognized as a national language by the Scottish Parliament.

However, it is clear that speaking in support of the definition of advocacy is not enough for charities. Yet in one sense it is easier to advocate for a theme or a change in the law. It is a safer space to operate in. More challenging is advocating on behalf of your own charity, especially if that involves funding and or a particular issue that has impacted on it.

Influencing

So, what influencing? Again, let us start with a dictionary definition. The Cambridge Dictionary states that influencing is 'to affect or change how someone or something develops, behaves, or thinks'.[2]

---

[2] Cambridge Dictionary, definition of *influence*. Available at: https://dictionary.cambridge.org/dictionary/english/influence [accessed 8 April 2022].

When charities talk about influencing, it is either in the context of what impacts on them as individual entities, or what impacts upon the sector. This section is going to concentrate on what influencing means in the context of an individual charity, and what the role of the board and trustees could, and should, be.

Much of the influencing that charities undertake can often be reactive to changes that could have a negative effect or restrict the charity's ability to pursue its purpose. The sector has a growing role as a key partner with national and local government, so knowing how to influence effectively is crucial. And whilst there is good work done by national membership organizations, it does not negate the need for each charity to have a clear sense of its influencing strategy.

How this strategy will be shaped will depend on a number of factors, whether you are a national or local charity, and if the issues are financial, policy or legislative. The answer will influence the shape of the actions to be taken. In my experience working with the sector over the last 30 years, two of the main areas affecting individual charities are local state funding and securing a level playing field for the commissioning of local services.

So what should the board do? Traditionally, it has been the CEO who has taken the main lead for the charity on local state funding and commissioning. This is someone who can talk with authority, but theirs is not the only voice that can and should be heard.

These are difficult matters to deal with and not for the faint-hearted. Individual charities are understandably reluctant to criticize or be seen to 'campaign' against local state funders. As tendering and commissioning are used as the main way to award contracts, charities are sensitive to accusations of 'lobbying'. Hence the need for clear processes for engagement and interactions. Trustees and boards can be reluctant to become exposed to local politics and engaging in public disagreements.

Yet there are some areas where boards and trustees can and should act. A good starting point is to accept that boards have a legitimate role in advocating and influencing on behalf of their purpose. Therefore, *an influencing strategy is a strategic necessity for a charity.* And in relation to influencing, the board should always be 'on'. Influencing should not just be turned to when things are difficult. This would be a missed opportunity and leaves power in the hands of funders.

For those dependent on funding from statutory agencies such as health and local authorities, the impact may be a reduction/closure in what the charity does. Board and trustees can play a key role in voicing their concerns and opposition. And whilst there may be benefits from speaking publicly and other campaigning techniques, in the first instance stick to private meetings. This is particularly important in the case of local authorities and elected members.

There are good tactical reasons for the use of boards in defensive campaigns. Not dependent on funding to pay their salary, they are able to speak their mind without any pecuniary conflict of interest. This means that they can engage with and challenge both officials and elected members without being compromised and say some of the things that a CEO might not want to say.

There is something powerful about board trustees speaking on behalf of their organizations and advocating for them. And it can have a positive effect on decision makers. As a city councillor, I was able to see the power of that influence first hand. The following case study will illustrate this point.

Case study

A social care charity that supported people with special needs had been given a 10% reduction in their council grant. In planning their response, the board made a strategic decision, which in hindsight was a masterclass in advocacy. It was agreed that Paolo, the Chair, would do most of the talking, backed up by other trustees rather than Sarah, the CEO. And rather than focusing on what it meant for the charity, making some staff redundant, the Chair and other trustees focused on the negative impact to the strategic priorities of the council by the cut.

The charity was a key provider in an area where there was not enough service and long waiting lists. It argued that it was counterproductive to cut the service, as it was a strategic priority and the consequences would be more expensive options that were contrary to the philosophical approach of the council.

After a lengthy conversation, the trustees convinced the council to rescind the decision. The decision was swung not just by the eloquence of the trustees, though they were well prepared, but that they took a risk arguing that the impact of the decision would have an even greater impact on the council than the charity itself. (Unlike the CEO arguing the case, where the accusation could be that it was about protecting their post and salary, no such charge can be laid against trustees who are unpaid volunteers with no pecuniary conflict of interest.)

In this case, by explaining the value of the specialist expertise of the charity, it helped reposition them from just being seen as a provider to a partner supporting the council with its strategic priorities. The lesson from the case study is not just to be prepared but ensure the board has a compelling narrative of what you do. In it show the difference it makes to citizens and at the same link it to how your charity is a critical element in other agencies delivering their strategic objectives.

Tip

These compelling narratives are a much more powerful way of getting the messages across to funders. By humanizing the story it makes it easier to engage in discussion. One of the ways that boards can do this is by providing examples of their work and the difference it makes. This can be best achieved by interviewing those who use the services on it how it has benefitted them; asking them to be part of a presentation is also another way of making it relevant and human.

It is wise for the board to establish an 'influence' at all levels of strategy. The development of a compelling narrative can be used by trustees in their networks to influence key decision makers. At the same time, it enables any members of staff or indeed service users to talk about what the charity means for them and the impact it makes.

The power of trustees focusing on the higher purpose of the organization can have greater influence in reshaping policy changes. As BoardSource puts it: 'the voice of the unpaid volunteer board member, acting or speaking out of altruism and passion for a worthy cause, is potentially much more influential than the highest-paid lobbyist. Never underestimate the impact that a volunteer board member [can have]'.[3]

Becoming an ambassadorial board

For those boards that have adopted an advocacy strategy, it is usually the Chair who 'faces up' such an approach. But it should not be restricted to the Chair. After all, it may be that the expert on a particular topic is not the Chair. So develop an approach that allows for all trustees to be comfortable in being ambassadors.

In designing a strategy, have regard for an internal audience and an external one. The external one – funders, legislators and supporters – is more familiar territory on which to develop. Less is thought of the role of trustees in relation to their internal audience, namely the staff and those who may use the services of the charity. So how should that work?

The relationship between the staff and the board can be a source of friction if there are not clear guidelines. In medium-sized organizations with a clear decision-making hierarchy this is easier to manage than in a small organization where they may be only one or two staff and the rest are volunteers. Let me focus on medium-sized and above.

As a rule, trustees should not be routinely and directly engaging with staff, and contact in relation to staff should be through the CEO. However, trustees visiting parts of the organization and hearing first hand from staff and those who use the service can be a good experience. It offers a clearer sense of what the organization does and the impact it makes. It offers

---

[3] BoardSource, *Ten Basic Responsibilities of Nonprofit Boards*, 2009. BoardSource website available at: https://boardsource.org/

a good grounding in what the organization is for, and it also consolidates trustees' own 'why'.

In terms of binding the organization together, it does no harm for staff to know who is on their board and what their interests are. Structured contact and visits to projects, talking to service users, helps broaden trustees' understanding. This awareness on specifics and tangibles moves board debates from the abstract to the actual.

So in preparing a strategy of external engagement, it is useful to map the networks that trustees have, their *circles of influence*. Outline them, cross reference them across the board membership and identify what connections or links they have with key decision makers. Such intelligence can be invaluable when planning a campaign to strengthen partnerships with statutory agencies.

Similarly, setting out a series of speaking engagements, at Rotaries, business associations, trade unions and other parts of civic society, can play a key role in awareness raising and the impact of the charity. It is here that the voluntary trustee can have more impact than the CEO. This use of 'soft power' is a good way to raise your charity's brand. Again, set-piece events where your charity invites decision makers, commissioners and funders to presentations on its work, lectures and seminars should ideally be led by the Chair, with the CEO.

These areas are easy to plan and implement. They help raise profile and build relationship and provide a structured way for trustees to develop their ambassadorial role.

Challenges

Dealing with statutory agencies can be challenging for charities, especially when much of the funding comes from them. Attempting to overturn or rescind a decision can be tough going and requires a great deal of thought before you go ahead. *Timing is key. Too often the decision to challenge is made too late to have any impact. So, the key objective of your strategy needs to be proactive and anticipatory.* That means getting to know who the key decision makers are and what makes them tick. Find out what challenges their organizations face, and how you can position yourself as an expert that can help their organization meet its objectives.

Get to understand their world and help them understand yours. And whilst much of that will be achieved through your primary contact, the CEO and senior staff working with their equivalents, there is an important role for the Chair and board trustees to develop relationships with decision makers. It is through these networks that trustees can play an advocacy and influencing role in a way that the CEO cannot.

If you have trustees on your board who feel comfortable advocating and influencing on behalf of your charity, well and good. If not, establishing a development programme for them would be a wise choice. After all, advocating and influencing is not just about preventing negative impacts, but rather about raising awareness of the positive impacts of your charity's interventions.

Conclusion

It may be an uncomfortable observation, but charities are operating in a competitive market. Whether it is competing with other charities in a commissioned/tendering environment for state funding, or for public donations, it requires a clear strategy and effective organizational implementation.

What is clear, however, is that relying solely on the CEO and the executive team to advocate is a missed opportunity. Wise charities will look to utilize the expertise of both the paid staff and the unpaid trustees. Indeed, providing the lead role for trustee has distinctive benefits, not least that they are distinctively placed to speak on behalf of the charity.

Encouraging trustees to reclaim advocate, influencer and ambassador roles brings an added value that is hard to replicate. Such a role is an empowering one for boards and trustees, and demonstrates them exercising their governance and leadership responsibilities, showing a board that is Governing with Purpose.

11 The learning board

Introduction

So how does a board become and operate as a learning board? It has to start with individual trustees' willingness to embrace continuous learning and development. Boards are often very passionate about the charities for which they serve. Yet of itself that passion is not enough. For without an understanding of your roles, and the ability to carry out them effectively as a trustee, you are little more than a supporter of a cause, not a leader. So a commitment to learning and development has the benefit of assisting you and your fellow trustees to be more effective in your leadership roles.

In promoting the learning board concept, there are two different facets that boards need to recognize. Firstly, the principle of a learning organization. This covers the whole of the organization and is led by the CEO. Most charities will have some form of that established. The second principle, which this chapter will focus on, is the principle of a learning board for trustees and the board. This should be initiated by the Chair, who has oversight responsibility for trustee and board training and development.

A strong and engaged board is a clear sign of a healthy one. Yet even the most effective of boards needs to review how well it is functioning in this fast-changing and uncertain environment. Good boards will repeatedly ask themselves how they can do better. They will check on how they are operating, review culture and behaviours, and establish practices for a healthy and engaged board.

It is often said that the strongest organizations have the strongest boards. However, that strength is not solely down to who is on the board but rather how the board operates.

Chapter aims

The aim of this chapter is to explain what a learning board is, identify approaches boards can use and outline the benefits to boards and trustees.

What is a learning board?

For a board committed to Governing with Purpose, continuous improvement to board governance is a central feature. Using the learning board approach can codify learning and development activity. In order to demonstrate the principles of a learning board, I have adapted Bob Garratt's Learning Board approach to design five key objectives to make it specific to the charity sector.[1]

- A 'learning' board acknowledges that governance and leadership are the core roles of board trustees.
- Being part of a learning board is about awareness in how you perform your role, with a desire to be the best you can be for the cause you care for. This requires a commitment to the principles of continuous improvement from both you and fellow trustees.
- Continuous improvement begins with acceptance of the importance of assessment and a review of individual and collective performance. A learning

---

[1] Bob Garratt, *The Fish Rots from the Head*, 2010, p. 236.

board adopts performance assessments not from a compliance perspective, but from a commitment to quality and high performance.

- These principles underpin the way in which the board attracts, recruits and develops existing board members.
- The learning board approach to continuous improvement and development recognizes the need for fresh faces, different voices and diversity of thought. Boards need to be able to regenerate and renew through making space for new appointments. Time limits on board membership address that.

Board value

The value of the learning board helps trustees visualize how to carry out their duties. In the widest context these roles are best seen as 'inside' the charity, for example ensuring purpose and ethos, scrutiny of performance, risk assessment and strategy, and 'outside' the charity, dealing with stakeholders, funders and responding to the external policy environment. This requires different skills and aptitudes from trustees. It is unreasonable to assume that all trustees will have all the requisite skills. Yet without any process of assessing that, the board is in the dark about whether their current skills match the challenges.

In turn, as a trustee, having the humility to be open about your development needs sends a powerful message to the rest of the organization. It is a visible demonstration of the board wanting to improve the governance of the charity.

This is an area where boards should be putting their emphasis; however, for a variety of reasons, it has not captured the imagination of board members, nor do they see it as a priority. For some boards there is a fear of exposure, realizing that they might not be as good as they think they are. Others demonstrate a complacent approach – summed up by a long-standing board member with the memorable phrase 'I am the finished article – what would I need with development?'

A consequence of the type of complacency referred to above is that there is little or no money and even less time spent on board development. Even if boards do not subscribe to the views above, there is a marked reluctance to spend on their own development. That needs to change. The fact that only 46% of charities had some form of board development speaks volumes.[2]

Boards committed to good governance practice already have a learning and development programme that enables them to be the best they can be. Smart boards will want to ensure they have a comprehensive model in place before regulators insist on it, or that funders may in the future require as a condition of funding.

Board development process

So, what should be a board development process look like? There are five key steps in that process. These are:

- To benchmark where they are, and where they want to be. The gap between is the basis of the learning and development programme. Without it there will be little meaningful progress.
- Every board member should have an annual development programme agreed with the Chair.
- The board must have a rigorous annual performance appraisal process. This should encompass two elements: self-assessment of individual trustees and evaluation of board performance.
- The process is overseen by the Chair, who is ultimately responsible for the performance of the board. And to keep faith with the process, the Chair should undergo a 360 led by an independent person.
- As well as lead the process, the Chair needs to reassure trustees as to the rationale behind the board development process, namely to improve the quality of governance of the charity, and encourage their involvement in shaping it.

---

[2] House of Lords Select Committee, 2017. Available at: https://publications.parliament.uk/pa/ld201617/ldselect/ldchar/133/13302.htm [accessed 8 April 2022].

Trustee self-assessment

For boards who are contemplating a development programme, a good place to start would be trustee self-assessment. Whereas staff and executive performance assessment would be the norm, the willingness of boards to engage in such a process is very variable.

A recent survey, *Leading with Intent*, stated that only a small majority (51%) of organizations reported that they use a formal, written self-assessment to evaluate their board's effectiveness.[3] It is surprising that against a backdrop of greater scrutiny and increased regulation more boards would not wish to assess their performance.

So, let me give you some reasons why board self-assessment is vital to effective governance. At the outset it is important to ground a learning board culture as a core value. How boards apply themselves also has a bearing. If driven by concerns to be compliant, that doesn't imply a thirst to be the best, but rather to pass a test. In effect, it becomes a tick-box exercise, resulting in little learning and no changes in behaviour. The converse is also true. The more committed the board is to learning, the better their governance and leadership will be. Some specific benefits of self-assessment are:

- the ability to reflect on their roles and responsibilities;
- self-identifying key strengths and challenges in fulfilling their role;
- indicating areas they enjoy less and require support with;
- highlighting their areas of interest and expertise;
- testing the extent of relationships with other trustees;
- providing intelligence to improve board team building.

Dealing with objections

And whilst the good practice arguments seem logical and sensible, it is important to recognize that trustees may be

---

[3] BoardSource, *Leading with Intent*, 2021. Available at: https://boardsource.org/wp-content/uploads/2021/06/2021-Leading-with-Intent-Report.pdf [accessed 8 April 2022].

resistant to an assessment process. There can be several reasons for reluctance, if not resistance.

- First and foremost, there is no culture of assessing trustee performance.
- Trustees are unclear about the purpose and do not see the link between their individual performance and that of the charity.
- Trustees believe they are doing a great job; assessment is not needed and would be a waste of time and energy.
- Some trustees are fearful that they will be blamed for the poor performance of others and that there is an 'agenda' to get rid of certain board members.
- The board is currently dealing with a crisis that requires its attention, and such a process would be a distraction to director focus.

Solutions to resistance

So, considering these objections, how do you get trustees to see the value to them and to their board?

The key is how the process is presented and communicated. It should be emphasized that the self-assessment process is a sense check on how each trustee feels about how they are carrying out their roles. It is not about blame or a league table on performance.

The first objective is to get commitment and 'buy-in'. The Chair has a crucial role to play in providing reassurance and explaining the rationale behind the process. This needs to be a real group effort with everyone involved. Without consensus, non-engagement and limited participation are the likely outcomes. Below is a list of suggested steps to follow:

- Agree what is going to be the basis of the questionnaire with all trustees.
- Seek an external facilitator to collect the questionnaires, analyse the contents and report to the board on findings.
- Guarantee confidentiality and ensure that their answers will not be attributed but aggregated into a report.

- Recognize it is the process that is important, not the answers.
- Provide each trustee with the opportunity to comment on how they assess their own performance.
- Finally, ensure action on issues raised is taken afterwards. No follow up is the worst consequence to self-assessment.

Guidance on developing self-assessment

Start by circulating some assessment templates (available online). This allows familiarity with what is involved and could be the basis for designing your own questions. Invite a charity that conducts self-assessment to speak to your board about how it operates and how it has benefitted trustees and the board. A template of standard questions is contained in Appendix 2 of this book.

> **Tip**
>
> Speak to other boards who have conducted trustee self-assessments and ask them to speak to your board about their experience.

Board evaluation

So how does a board measure its own effectiveness?

Boards have well-established processes for measuring the effectiveness of the charity they oversee. Some of them will have been determined by external regulators, others internally driven by organizational considerations. Yet regarding the performance of boards themselves, there is huge variation in how boards measure the effectiveness of their performance, with some choosing not to. And from a trustee perspective the opportunity to know how you perform both as an individual and as a member of the board can bring insights.

Culture, 'the way we do things here', is critical to setting the tone for organizational effectiveness. Boards and trustees need to understand that how they set that tone, create that culture and establish relationships with the CEO and executive team has a direct impact on whether the charity will be successful in achieving its purpose. Evaluation enables the board to discern whether the impact of their behaviours is contributing to the success of the organization or getting in the way.

There are number of online resources that can be used to develop your evaluation, but before embarking on a board evaluation, be clear what you want to achieve from the evaluation.

Benefits for the board

Firstly, it is good practice. It shows that the board is committed to improving the effectiveness of board governance.

It sends a message that the board is not beyond and above rules, where everyone else in the charity must undergo appraisal except the board.

It enables the board to be aligned with the rest of the charity and provides a powerful impulse of shared experience. This has crucial role to play in building morale.

It provides intelligence on how the alignment (or not) between board matters and those of the charity impacts on the charity.

It provides a sense check on where the board's interests and expertise lie, allowing for strengthening particular areas.

It offers an insight into how board trustees are working together and how the machinery of governance is working.

As in all processes, how the objective of the evaluation is articulated and how the learnings are shared are of critical importance. It needs to be safe for trustees to speak their truth; therefore, confidentiality is crucial and trust in the process paramount. This is best achieved by using an external and independent person to conduct the evaluation. This makes it easier for trustees who are reluctant to 'tell all' or express concerns about the behaviour of the Chair.

In larger charities there may be a governance committee that would initiate the action, but to ensure confidence in the process it is important that the Chair does not conduct the evaluation, but rather endorses the principle and ensures it is resourced.

Conclusion

So, in conclusion, making Governing with Purpose a set of behaviours requires it to be practised and celebrated by boards. The principle of a learning board is intrinsic to that and therefore needs to be championed by trustees. For the principle of continuous improvement to be genuinely adopted, it must be an intrinsic motivation for trustees who want to be better in their role. On that basis, it will have a greater stickability than extrinsic motivation driven by exhortation or compliance models.

The Chair has a particular responsibility to embody and uphold the practice of a learning board in their everyday actions. It is an approach that is challenging; however, it brings together the three core relationships and accountabilities of governance: What does the Chair expect of the board and vice versa? What does the CEO expect of the Chair and vice versa? And finally, what does the board expect of the CEO and vice versa? This helps to bridge the different roles and responsibilities of trustees and paid staff and recognize the symbiotic relationship between the two. How these relations play out determines the quality of the governance and leadership displayed by the board.

In turn, the learning board approach allows trustees to realize that governing is not a series of distinct events which are switched on and off, but rather that the leadership of governance is an organic flow of activities that relate with and link to one another. And for that trustees and boards need to be adaptable. However as Abraham Maslow said in 1966, 'I suppose it is tempting, if the only tool you have is a hammer, to treat everything as if it were a nail'.[4] Therefore, to be adaptable boards need to embrace continuous improvement for effective governance and leadership.

Not all boards have such a commitment to continuous improvement of their effectiveness. That is a pity. Trustees who feel that way place a credibility gap between themselves and the rest of the organization over which they have oversight. It sends an implicit, if not explicit, message that learning and development is for everyone else but not for us. This can be read by employees as 'we trustees don't need it' or 'we are not interested in learning'. Either way, it creates a dissonance between the leaders and the led. This in turn impacts on trust and respect.

Instead, a learning board solidifies these relationships around mutual respect, understanding of expertise, an awareness of accountabilities, recognition of different stresses and, above all, a shared and common purpose. That is Governing with Purpose.

---

[4] Abraham Maslow, The Psychology of Science: A Reconnaissance, 1966. HarperCollins, p. 15.

12 Recruit and renew

Introduction

For a board committed to Governing with Purpose, it all begins with recruitment, onboarding and retention (or if necessary, removal) of the right trustees. In turn, the board needs to understand the central role that recruitment plays in upskilling, renewing and making the board more representative of the communities it serves.

Directing and guiding that falls squarely on trustees. How that process is managed and those selected from it may well outlive your involvement with the board, so succession planning should be undertaken wisely and with the best interests of the charity in mind.

Chapter aims

The aim of this chapter is to emphasize the importance of recruitment, succession planning and board renewal. It will outline the critical role of trustees in directing the process and will highlight some key approaches for success.

Recruitment strategy

So how does your board go about such a process? Let's start with first principles. Good boards will want to ensure that those who replace them will be better skilled, better equipped and more diverse than they were. Leaving a legacy of continuous improvement is one specific way in which trustees can measure their impact on succession planning, including a rigorous recruitment strategy.

Across the sector, there is a wide range of recruitment strategies, some of which are questionable as to their effectiveness. Despite that, there has been significant progress from the days when the CEO or Chair produced a list of people, who were best classed as 'helping a friend out' appointments. That is not to say that these individuals did not perform a role, but the process was opaque to say the least, with all the attributes of an old boy's club and resulted in more people like them.

Since then, the approach has varied from advertising vacancies on recruitment websites to seeking referrals from existing board trustees. Some larger organizations hand over the process to head-hunters to attract candidates. The breadth of approaches demonstrates a lack of consistency across the sector, though some of that may be in relation to the size of individual charities.

Therefore, the recruitment strategy needs to be informed by something wider than the need to replace someone whose changed circumstances mean they can no longer participate in the board. Such a reactive approach is no longer sustainable for one of the most important decisions a board will make, namely who it appoints to a board. It needs to be more thorough, consistent and professional. And with the overriding aim of seeking better than the existing board. It is that ambition that will take the board to where it needs to be.

It is said that your performance is only as good as your team – so how your board is recruited, developed and supported goes to the heart of Governing with Purpose. It should not involve replacing like for like. As Marshall Goldsmith puts it, 'what got you here won't get you there'.[1] Deciding on what types of trustees are required should be based on strengthening and developing the board both individually and collectively.

So, what is the balance of capabilities and competencies that the board need to encompass? Boards need to get better at reflecting the diversity of the communities and stakeholders they serve. We tend to recruit in our own image and likeness, so there needs to be a conscious decision to do it differently if a wider pool of applicants is to be sought and recruited. It also needs to recognize that in response to changing themes, cybersecurity and digitization being two obvious ones, trustees experienced in these specialist areas may be required in the boardroom.

There is a temptation for charities to seek lawyers, HR specialists and accountants, for example, to sit on their boards as a 'two for one' approach, namely they get free advice as well as the governance experience. Such a move is misguided. Trustees should be appointed because of their governance and leadership capabilities, not as a means of accessing free specialist advice.

> **Tip**
>
> Be clear what you are recruiting for – is it a skills gap (for example, a trustee who has extensive experience in leading charity mergers) or a representational gap (for example, where the charity operates in a diverse community yet the board are all white middle-aged males).

The actual process of recruitment should evidence the board's values, practising what it preaches. A good place to start is seeking out those who are underrepresented on boards. Adopting approaches such as 'apprentice' board members or 'shadowing', which have been successful in other parts of the world, shows your board's willingness to take risks and reach out to a wider reservoir of talent.

---

[1] Marshall Goldsmith, *What Got You Here Won't Get You There*, 2008. Profile Books.

Boards also benefit from diversity of thought and challenge. After all, diversity/iconoclasm is a good counterweight to groupthink, as we highlighted in Chapter 8. And boards that take risks exposing themselves to people with different opinions have greater depth and capacity to make better decisions.

When boards don't just make these in principle decisions to support diversity but actually recruit from communities demonstrating their diversity, this advocacy cannot not be underestimated. The symbolism of intentions becoming actions is a powerful message to stakeholders, funders and potential board trustees. So if your board is serious about attracting the best and diverse, hire professional recruiters to organize the process. This is a competitive field with many charities seeking the best, so getting the right fit between the board and candidates is crucial.

Onboarding

A clear induction process is vital for continuity between selection and taking up the role. It needs to involve more than simply giving new trustees a handbook and copies of the articles of association. A good onboarding process should cover:

- ethos – what we stand for;
- behaviour – 'the way we do things here'.

It should introduce new trustees to the principle of a learning board, and the board's commitment to collective and individual continuous improvement.

The induction process needs to start with an unambiguous definition of the legal responsibility of the individual trustee, highlighting mutual responsibility for your own actions and those of your fellow trustees. As outlined in Chapter 1, the terminology of trustees, board members and board directors is used interchangeably, and as a result, there can be a tendency within the charity sector to assume that the legal responsibilities of a trustee differ from those of a company director. They do not. Trustees are as equally liable as private company directors for wrongdoing, which can result in a charity being wound up and trustees being disbarred.

So in the context of Governing with Purpose, it is important that new trustees are aware of the onerous nature of their responsibilities, not just for themselves, but equally importantly for the cause that the charity serves. And on that basis, they need to be sufficiently self-aware, or if not, sufficiently self-interested, to seek professional development in their role, and insist that their colleagues undertake similar development.

Onboarding should introduce new trustees to the principle of a learning board, and the board's commitment to collective and individual continuous improvement. It should reflect the diverse needs of the board, stretching from training, such as on how to read a balance sheet, to personal development, such as developing confidence. In turn, if boards are serious about instituting a learning board approach, it will require resources and funding. A Governing with Purpose board will regard this as an investment rather than a drain.

Term limits

At some stage, it will be time for board trustees to move on. Being a trustee can take its toll. Some have been there for too long and have lost interest; others feel they want to leave but don't want to let their colleagues down by resigning. Often there are a lot of emotions attached to being on a board. However, we all have a 'sell by' date and good trustees will know theirs. Yet unless there is a clear process, seeking removal can be messy.

A Governing with Purpose board will be wedded to the principles of board renewal. Setting a cap on the amount of time a trustee can serve without having to seek reappointment or re-election is an important principle.

Term limits concentrate minds, provide opportunities for renewal and enable a planned approach to succession planning. It is no coincidence that many countries have time limits on presidential terms, as do many public/state appointments.

These are designed to act as a restraint on the misuse of power, or more generally a sense of 'entitlement' that unconsciously envelopes even the most benign.

It also implicitly recognizes that there are limits to effectiveness, and that the very nature of governance and leadership is a demanding one. Therefore, there is a safety valve to minimize burnout – and also to introduce fresh and new voices. Not least to respond to the long-overdue need for boards to reflect the diversity of the communities they serve.

And like any other role, it can be routine and repetitive. Indeed, you can begin to question if you are really making a difference. All these thoughts are common, and it is important that you are satisfied in your role. Frankly speaking, boards do not need saints or martyrs, but fully functioning trustees who have strong personal insight. Introducing term limits allows board members to focus on what they want to achieve during their period in office.

Case study

Eric was a long-term member of a local credit union. He was stagnating in his role and had little real involvement. He refused to go on training courses, stating that 'he had plenty of experience'. The Chair, Yasmin, was unhappy with his contribution and received complaints from fellow trustees, but Eric continued to stay on because he didn't think that there would be anyone to replace him. Other than a vote of no confidence in him, which was unlikely, it was Feargal as CEO who was in the best position to determine Eric's position on the board. New regulations on financial competence for board members were soon to be introduced and Feargal knew that Eric would struggle to meet the level of competence required. As it transpired, Eric did resign. There was no difficulty in getting a replacement.

Term limits of themselves do not solve all issues; however, in the context of Governing with Purpose they have several benefits.

- They provide a way to avoid the stagnation, boredom and loss of commitment that long-serving trustees can sometimes exhibit.
- They avoid domination by long timers who, if left unchecked, can intimidate contrary voices.
- They provide a way to remove those passive, poorly performing or troublesome board members in a dignified and business-like manner.

Some considerations

Whilst the benefits of term limits far exceed the negatives, it is important to recognize some of those negative effects. Term times need to be realistic to allow trustees to become effective in their governance role and avoid uncertainty through constant turnover of short term limits.

To minimize disruption, ensure that term limits are staggered. It is best to avoid an 'all in all out' approach. This leads to unnecessary lag time as the new board learn their roles. A staggered approach allows for continuity yet at the same time brings fresh ideas and changes the dynamic.

It would be best to draw a distinction between term limits for trustees and the Chair. The two-term limit (with a term of three years) for a Chair will prevent too much concentration of power. If the organization is a membership body, each term should be ratified (or not) through an AGM. If it is not a membership body, the term limits should be set out in the articles of association of the charity.

Term limits are not a magical wand to improve and revitalize a board, but they can contribute to the quality and performance of board governance.

Conclusion

Once a board is clear that the primary purpose of trustees is leadership and governance, it becomes much easier to plan for recruitment and renewal. It means that succession planning is integral to board and trustee development from the outset.

It enables trustees to start thinking about what they want to achieve during their time on the board, in turn giving more focus to how they use their skills and expertise and to what effect.

This creates a common culture within the board which is less impacted by the behaviour of dominant individuals or issues that can distract. At the same time, effective recruitment strategies and removal structures via term limits provide a safety valve and a means to introduce better-equipped and more diverse trustees to a governance role.

Conclusion

Congratulations if you are reading this sentence. It means you have stuck with me throughout the book. If you have discovered nothing else, you have demonstrated stamina, patience and perseverance. Attributes that are valuable around the board governance table.

In the time from when I started to write this book to completing it in March 2022, much of what we understood about the environment of work has changed beyond all recognition. Organizations are grappling with working from home and hub, hybrid working has become the norm. Whilst the end of the office has been overstressed, workplace culture is going to be very different as we adapt to a changing public environment, staff expectations of a better work–life balance, and the dramatic growth and use of communications technology.

Nowhere is this more evident in the charity sector, especially those providing human services either in a centre or in individuals' homes. Charities have turned their organizations inside to enable them to support service users and fulfil their purpose. COVID-19 has put a huge strain on boards and trustees, who are fearful about the financial future, wanting to ensure a duty of care for staff and for those who the charity supports, and striving to provide effective governance to sustain their charity through unforeseen and unprecedented events. The very fact that most of the sector has survived, if somewhat shaken, points to a level of resilience within the operational performance and governance of charities.

External environment

As society adapts to the realities of living in a post-COVID-19 world, the pressure on charities to improve their performance in relation to services that they have won through tender, or have been given through the state, means that funders will continue to impose exacting standards on how that money is spent, whilst at the same expecting 'more for less'. In terms of measuring the quality of services provided, by all the likelihood this will also attract higher and more demanding standards, as it rightly should. The challenge for boards is whether to stick with compliance frameworks as directed or use them to develop a commitment model that puts quality at the heart of everything the board does.

It provides an opportunity to reposition your charity and gain a reputation for commitment to the highest-quality standards. And in the competitive market in which charities compete with each other for funding, unpalatable as it may be for you as reader, it creates a niche. To take such an approach will impact on the board's governance as well as operational compliance, and as such requires a strategic decision to be taken.

Change in the boardroom

It is already clear from the external environment that 'business as usual' is no longer possible, nor should it be desirable. Boards need to up their governance, both to respond to what is going on in the outside, but equally importantly about how they actually *govern*. And that requires a recalibration of the relationship between the CEO/executive team and board trustees. Developing the governance as leadership model brings greater capacity and expertise of trustees along with the executive to formulate better policy and co-design strategy. That new relationship across governance rather than in silos is helped in no small measure by the binding qualities of generative work highlighted in Chapter 9.

This will have the benefit of giving an answer to the almost 1 million trustees in the UK who give up their time for free, and who hitherto have been concerned with whether they were making a difference.

The boardroom will need to reflect on new challenges that require addressing cyber security threats, or the new requirement for boards to have environmentally friendly and carbon-neutral policies in response to new regulations around Environmental Social Governance (ESG).

Better governance

As a board trustee, how do you know you are effective? This is a common question posed by consultants and authors to those sitting on charity boards. Yet when the question is asked of the CEO and executive team they can rattle off a series of metrics that evidence their performance.

So what can trustees do? Well, for a start they can identify ways to make board meetings more effective by introducing the 12-month agenda; developing working relationships with the CEO beyond the board meeting as a way to ask questions and deal with detail would make a significant impact.

Encouraging better systems of delegating to committees or short life groups containing executives and trustees is a way of discussing complex issues outside a formal deliberative forum. However, most boards and trustees seem to be more comfortable in their scrutiny role, looking backwards; holding the CEO to account gives a tangible sense of activity, whereas for some strategy can be seen as intangible.

Trustees need to make a step change away from such attitudes. It allows for too much refuge in detail and disempowers trustees who end up competing in a memory test with the CEO. Instead, trusts should shift their focus to leadership. Trustees need to realise that they are more powerful than they realise, and therefore to 'own' that power and use it to lead and govern well for causes they care about. They need to be bold in asserting their leadership role.

Building relationships

The CEO/Chair relationship is the core relationship that binds together (or not) the organization and the board. And whilst it is good if they both like each other, that is not required for them to work well together. What is required is mutual respect, clarity on roles and responsibilities, and a process for dealing with points of difference.

That relationship can set the tone for how the board operates, but the board does not need to mirror or imitate bad behaviour; indeed, as keepers of the flame, protecting the ethos and purpose of the charity should push back on behaviours that negatively impact on board performance. Trustees have a critical role in creating an environment where all voices are heard and all trustees are listened to. It is through these actions that trustees make the ethos of the charity a real thing rather than a well-meaning intention.

Smarter decision making

The lessons learned from dealing with the pandemic and making difficult choices regarding resourcing, staffing and development over the last few years mean that in order to plan ahead, boards need more creative and agile ways to make decisions, especially awkward and difficult ones.

And because of the uncertain environment, boards need to ensure that the willingness to seek consensus on decisions for a cause/charity that is cared for doesn't become a case of loyalty trumping questioning. The dangers of slipping into groupthink should always be at the forefront of trustees' minds. That is why some of the new approaches to assessing and ranking decisions before making them, outlined in Chapter 6, break with the binary for or against. This results in a safer space for trustees to express their views and rank options, which can be a valuable tool when faced with a series of difficult choices.

Inclusion and diversity

There needs to be a big push to get boards to be more representative – but for that to happen boards need to act at both ends of the board journey. Firstly, boards need to be more creative and proactive in planting the seed of leadership within the communities they serve, and find fresh ways to attract individuals who would not immediately think of joining a board.

Apprentice board trustee models have been very successful in providing safe spaces for experiencing the reality of boardroom life. Examples of trustees speaking to groups in their communities about what board life is like and what making a difference looks like are all great ways of raising awareness of the possibility that a seat on a charity board might be something for them.

And for those who express an interest, connecting with a mentor in advance of being appointed to a board will help in preparing and reducing the fear factor, enabling individuals to be board ready.

At the other end of the spectrum, the recruitment and onboarding process, boards need to up their game in becoming more diverse and more attractive to a wider range of people. Why is this important? Post pandemic, there has been a renaissance in volunteering and personal development. Together these two themes have inspired many to give something back and find something fulfilling beyond work.

This means that there are a lot of motivated potential board trustees out there; many are very clear about what they want, and it is a competitive environment for potential trustees. So smart boards will ensure their commitment to an ethos that espouses diversity can be matched by actions. How the board position their purpose and are welcoming to all needs to be explicit throughout the recruitment process.

Renewal

Which brings us to board renewal. With so many charities not having term limits, it is difficult to succession plan and to recruit for diversity; these plans depend on a dead person's shoes. The lack of term limits does test the legitimacy of a board of governance, leading to accusations of a self-selecting and self-perpetuating group. And whilst that charge is well wide of the mark in my experience, a reluctance to change may start to give it credence.

Being on a board is both a privilege and sometimes a burden. Trustees can get to the position where they are burnt out and have little left to give. In this instance they are not giving of their best; however, it is not fair that the trustees should be in that position. Term limits are not the sole answer to board renewal but do give guardrails to trustees on how to manage and plan their period on the board. It allows for trustees to leave with dignity and respect, at a time of their choosing, and to be recognized for their contribution.

It allows for succession planning in a methodical way and is an ideal opportunity to bring fresh and different faces to the board. Many of these individuals may have been part of the apprentice campaign or been attracted to high-profile requests for those who are historically underrepresented on charity boards. Either way, it is a start that is long overdue.

The learning principle

The proposals outlined above can only be fully realized if the board as a collective, and trustees individually, understand that a Governing with Purpose board demonstrates its commitment to continuous learning. That is a commitment to both the trustees and to the board as whole. As leaders, trustees need to be seen to be subject to the same principles that staff are, namely performance appraisal and personal and professional development, to enable them to be more effective for the charity they serve. As keepers of the flame, it is expected of trustees that they will be ambitious for themselves and for their charity to be the best they can be.

Again, a board driven by the principles of learning and continuous improvement will build greater capacity and resilience both within the board and by extension the rest of the organization.

Finally, the near future is uncertain, as near futures usually are. What is predictable is that charities are not going to be less needed any time soon. Whether the space that charities currently inhabit will continue to grow or be challenged by private for-profit companies, especially in the field of social care, is another uncertainty. What is not uncertain is that boards practising governance and leadership, Governing with Purpose, will be in a stronger position to hold their own.

Appendix 1

Trustees' six main duties[1]

1. Ensure your charity is carrying out its purposes for the public benefit

You and your co-trustees must make sure that the charity is carrying out the purposes for which it is set up, and no other purpose. This means you should:

- ensure you understand the charity's purposes as set out in its governing document;
- plan what your charity will do, and what you want it to achieve;
- be able to explain how all of the charity's activities are intended to further or support its purposes;
- understand how the charity benefits the public by carrying out its purposes.

---

[1] Guidance taken from Charity Commission for England and Wales, *The Essential Trustee: What You Need to Know, What You Need to Do*, 2018. Available at: www.gov.uk/government/publications/the-essential-trustee-what-you-need-to-know-cc3/the-essential-trustee-what-you-need-to-know-what-you-need-to-do [accessed 8 April 2022].

Spending charity funds on the wrong purposes is a very serious matter; in some cases, trustees may have to reimburse the charity personally.

2. Comply with your charity's governing document and the law

You and your co-trustees must:

- make sure that the charity complies with its governing document;
- comply with charity law requirements and other laws that apply to your charity.

You should take reasonable steps to find out about legal requirements, for example by reading relevant guidance or taking appropriate advice when you need to.

Registered charities must keep their details on the register up to date and ensure they send the right financial and other information to the commission in their annual return or annual update.

Find out more about your governing document and the law.

3. Act in your charity's best interests

You must:

- do what you and your co-trustees (and no one else) decide will best enable the charity to carry out its purposes;
- with your co-trustees, make balanced and adequately informed decisions, thinking about the long term as well as the short term;
- avoid putting yourself in a position where your duty to your charity conflicts with your personal interests or loyalty to any other person or body;
- not receive any benefit from the charity unless it's properly authorized and is clearly in the charity's interests; this also includes anyone who is financially connected to you, such as a partner, dependent child or business partner.

4. Manage your charity's resources responsibly

You must act responsibly, reasonably and honestly. This is sometimes called the duty of prudence. Prudence is about exercising sound judgement. You and your co-trustees must:

- make sure the charity's assets are only used to support or carry out its purposes;
- not take inappropriate risks with the charity's assets or reputation;
- not over-commit the charity;
- take special care when investing or borrowing;
- comply with any restrictions on spending funds.

You and your co-trustees should put appropriate procedures and safeguards in place and take reasonable steps to ensure that these are followed. Otherwise you risk making the charity vulnerable to fraud or theft, or other kinds of abuse, and being in breach of your duty.

5. Act with reasonable care and skill

As someone responsible for governing a charity, you:

- must use reasonable care and skill, making use of your skills and experience and taking appropriate advice when necessary;
- should give enough time, thought and energy to your role, for example by preparing for, attending and actively participating in all trustees' meetings.

6. Ensure your charity is accountable

You and your co-trustees must comply with statutory accounting and reporting requirements. You should also:

- be able to demonstrate that your charity is complying with the law, is well run and effective;
- ensure appropriate accountability to members, if your charity has a membership separate from the trustees;
- ensure accountability within the charity, particularly where you delegate responsibility for particular tasks or decisions to staff or volunteers.

Making decisions as a trustee

Charity trustees make decisions about their charity together, working as a team. Decisions don't usually need to be unanimous as long as the majority of trustees agree. They're usually made at charity meetings.

When you and your co-trustees make decisions about your charity, you must:

- act within your powers;
- act in good faith, and only in the interests of your charity;
- make sure you are sufficiently informed, taking any advice you need;
- take account of all relevant factors you are aware of;
- ignore any irrelevant factors;
- deal with conflicts of interest and loyalty;
- make decisions that are within the range of decisions that a reasonable trustee body could make in the circumstances.

You should record how you made more significant decisions in case you need to review or explain them in the future.[2]

Chair and Treasurer trustee roles

Some trustees have special roles, such as the Chair and the Treasurer. They are known as officers. You must comply with any specific provisions in your governing document about officers. Officers don't automatically have any extra powers or legal duties than the other trustees, but may carry out specific roles or have specific responsibilities delegated to them. Don't forget: all trustees remain jointly responsible for the charity.

---

[2] For more information see, Charity Commission for England and Wales, *It's Your Decision: Charity Trustees and Decision Making*, 2013. Available at: www.gov.uk/government/publications/its-your-decision-charity-trustees-and-decision-making/its-your-decision-charity-trustees-and-decision-making [accessed 8 April 2022].

For example, all trustees share responsibility for finances (not just the Treasurer).[3]

When trustees can be personally liable

It's extremely rare, but not impossible, for charity trustees to be held personally liable:

- to their charity, if they cause a financial loss by acting improperly;
- to a third party that has a legal claim against the charity, which the charity can't meet.

Understanding potential liabilities will help you to protect yourself and your charity by taking action to reduce the risk. This includes complying with your duties. It also includes deciding whether your charity should become incorporated (for example, as a company or CIO).[4]

---

[3] Find out more about Chair and Treasurer roles: www.gov.uk/government/publications/the-essential-trustee-what-you-need-to-know-cc3/the-essential-trustee-what-you-need-to-know-what-you-need-to-do#s12 [accessed 8 April 2022]

[4] More information about reducing the risk of liability is available at: www.gov.uk/government/publications/the-essential-trustee-what-you-need-to-know-cc3/the-essential-trustee-what-you-need-to-know-what-you-need-to-do#s10, while information on helping to run a charity is available at: www.gov.uk/government/get-involved/take-part/help-run-a-charity [accessed 8 April 2022].

Appendix 2

Trustees' self-assessment template

Choose a number corresponding to your answer (5 = completely; 4 = to a great extent; 3 = to some extent; 2 = a little extent; 1 = not at all).

Question	1	2	3	4	5
To what extent are you able to regularly attend scheduled board meetings?					
To what extent would you prepare in advance of board meetings, e.g. reading papers and supporting documents, asking questions?					
To what extent are you able to engage with and discuss all the board topics effectively?					
Do you have a conflict of interest that limits your board contribution/effectiveness?					
To what extent do you keep an open mind on all the issues being discussed?					

How easily do you engage with fellow board members?					
How easily do you get on with the Chair?					
How easily do you find it to engage with the CEO and senior management team?					
To what extent do you understand what governing actually means?					
How well do you think you govern?					
To what extent can you demonstrate evidence of your ability to carry out your roles and responsibilities?					
How easily do you find it to make a least one contribution at the board meeting?					
To what extent have you an understanding of the field in which your charity operates?					
To what extent would you wish further development, mentoring and support to strengthen you in your role?					

Bibliography

Bain, Neville (2008). *The Effective Director*. Director Publications Ltd.

Chait, Richard P., Ryan, William P. and Taylor, Barbara E. (2005). *Governance as Leadership: Reframing the Work of Nonprofit Boards*. John Wiley & Sons, Inc.

Charam, Ram (2005). *Boards that Deliver: Advancing Corporate Governance from Compliance to Competitive Advantage*. John Wiley & Sons, Inc.

Covey, Stephen M.R. with Merrill, Rebecca (2006). *The Speed of Trust: The One Thing that Changes Everything*. Simon & Schuster.

Dunne, Patrick (2021). *Boards*. Governance Publishing and Information Services Ltd.

Garratt, Bob (2010). *The Fish Rots from the Head: Developing Effective Board Directors*. Profile Books Ltd.

Heffernan, Margaret (2020). *Uncharted: How Uncertainty Can Power Change*. Simon & Schuster.

Janis, Irving (1982). *Victims of Groupthink* (2nd ed.). Houghton Mifflin.

Marquet, L. David. (2013). *Turn the Ship Around! A True Story of Building Leaders by Breaking the Rules*. Portfolio.

Meadows, Donella H. (2008). *Thinking in Systems: A Primer* (Wright, Diana, ed.). Chelsea Green Publishing.

Mintzberg, Henry (1994). *The Rise and Fall of Strategic Planning.* Free Press and Prentice Hall International.

Nadler, David, Behan, Beverly A. and Nadler, Mark B. (eds) (2006). *Building Better Boards: A Blueprint for Effective Governance.* Jossey-Bass.

Rumelt, Richard (2017). *Good Strategy/Bad Strategy: The Difference and Why It Matters.* Profile Books Ltd.

Spiegelhalter, David (2019). *The Art of Statistics: How to Learn from Data.* Penguin Random House.

Syed, Matthew (2015). *Black Box Thinking: The Surprising Truth About Success.* John Murray Publishers.

Syed, Matthew (2019). *Rebel Ideas: The Power of Diverse Thinking.* John Murray Publishers.

Acknowledgements

It has taken a long time to get here, and I couldn't have done it on my own. As soon as you start to write you realize that a book is a team effort, and I have been lucky to have had a large team.

Most of my career has been in and around the boardroom table or in the committee room. Whether as board member, trusted advisor or mentor to boards, it has brought me into contact with a wide range of people and different views on what good governance looks like. This has enabled me to have conversations and share experiences with many people involved in board governance, for which I am grateful. These conversations have helped shaped some of my thinking that has formed this book.

In specific terms I would like to thank everyone who read through the draft and helped it to get ready for editing. Their comments and observations have made the material much more readable. Special thanks to Karen McDowell, who patiently deciphered my bad handwriting into typed words.

I'd like to thank the staff at Newgen Publishing UK for their work on the production of the book, particularly Dr Lizzie Evans, Senior Production Editor. Special thanks to Katie Finnegan, whose skilful editing has made the book readable. Thanks also to Judith Wise, Marketing Manager at Practical Inspiration Publishing.

Yet without Alison Jones and Practical Inspiration Publishing this book would still be sitting in the 'to-do' pile. It was first suggested to me that I should write a book on boards at least five or six years ago, and whilst passionate about the subject, I was unable to take it much further.

Attending a ten-day workshop led by Alison on how to write a book gave me the structure and confidence to turn my thoughts and views from my head to paper. That continued support and guidance gave me the confidence to start, finish and, above all, enjoy the book writing experience.

I hope you enjoy the book as much as I enjoyed writing it.

About the author

For over 30 years, Brian Cavanagh has been involved in governance and leadership. He has extensive experience of governance and decision making, including 17 years as a city councillor and 10 years as a non-executive director and Chair of Scotland's second largest health authority.

A passionate advocate of empowering boards, he acts as a trusted advisor and governance specialist to CEOs and the boards of many leading charities in the UK and Ireland. Brian is also Chair of a SME in Scotland and sits on the board of an Irish housing association.

Brian lives in Ireland.

Index

Figures are indicated by *italics* and tables by **bold type**. Footnotes are indicated by the page number followed by "n" and the footnote number e.g., 97n4 refers to footnote 4 on page 97.